UFOs
in
Pennsylvania

Encounters with Extraterrestrials
in the Keystone State

Patty A. Wilson

STACKPOLE
BOOKS

Copyright ©2011 by Stackpole Books

Published by
STACKPOLE BOOKS
5067 Ritter Road
Mechanicsburg, PA 17055
www.stackpolebooks.com

All rights reserved, including the right to reproduce this book or portions thereof in any form or by any means, electronic or mechanical, including photocopying, recording, or by any information storage and retrieval system, without permission in writing from the publisher. All inquiries should be addressed to Stackpole Books.

Printed in the United States of America

10 9 8 7 6 5 4 3 2 1

FIRST EDITION

Cover design by Caroline Stover

Cover illustration by Marc Radle

Library of Congress Cataloging-in-Publication Data

Wilson, Patty A.
    UFOs in Pennsylvania : encounters with extraterrestrials in the Keystone State / Patty A. Wilson. — 1st ed.
        p. cm.
    Includes bibliographical references.
    ISBN-13: 978-0-8117-0648-3 (pbk.)
    ISBN-10: 0-8117-0648-6 (pbk.)
    1. Unidentified flying objects—Sightings and encounters—Pennsylvania.
I. Title.
    TL789.5.P4W55 2011
    001.94209748—dc22
                                    2010044981

Contents

O f all the bizarre phenomena that have happened in Pennsylvania, encounters with unidentified flying objects (UFOs) are the most terrifying. Ghosts and cryptozoological creatures simply don't carry the horror that alien beings do.

Everyone is familiar with the idea of strange lights or odd craft seen in the night skies, but Pennsylvania's UFO reports go far beyond that. They are many and varied. It seems that strange beings are stalking the people of the Keystone State.

As my work on this book progressed, I began to see patterns in the sightings. Many people spoke of feeling disconnected and unable to exert their own will when faced with a UFO. They felt compelled to follow whatever their strange captors told them to do. There were similarities in the types of beings, too. In fact, I would find three cases from separate areas, handled by different investigators, that had never been published. Those three cases all described the same being. That was just creepy!

Personally, I spent many sleepless nights working on this book. I found myself looking at the sky differently and apprehensively as the book progressed. I began to understand the creeping fear and the determination that abductees and many witnesses exhibited. They were determined to cope with and understand what had happened to them.

I have often been asked if anything rattles me. I usually say that nothing really frightens me. I've spent countless nights in haunted houses and checked up on crypto creatures, but I will have to change my answer now. UFOs and alien beings do scare me, and they'll scare you, too, after you read this book.

Sky Sightings

The most common type of UFO sighting is that of strange lights in the sky. Judging from the reports I've gathered here, there are some very bizarre things in the heavens above us. Be prepared for what you might see if you look up!

THE DIVIDING UFO

Nancy drove through the darkness of the late November night in 1998, keeping an eye out her windshield for deer. She had lived in the area for most of her life, and she watched the familiar countryside flash by in the headlights. Nancy was driving through a rural section of Washington County along with her eight-year-old daughter, Landy, who was rattling on as children do. The girl was chatting with her mom while looking out the window and would occasionally break into song.

Suddenly a bright amber star glowed brightly in the sky in front of the car.

"Mommy," Landy called. "Do you see the pretty star?"

Nancy slowed the car down and gazed, awestruck, through the windshield. A large amber light twinkled among the blue-white stars in the black velvet sky. The amber star was much larger than the other stars, though.

Nancy came to a wide spot and pulled over in the turnaround. She grabbed her purse and fumbled for her eyeglasses in the pouch where she always kept them. She rarely wore them to drive, but now she wanted to see the amber light better.

Nancy couldn't immediately find the glasses, so she flipped on the overhead dome light. She grabbed the glasses and pushed them on quickly. Landy gasped beside her and Nancy turned her gaze back toward the sky.

The amber light had begun to pulse red, yellow, blue, green, white, and back to amber; the pulsing picked up until the star gave off a multicolored strobe effect.

Whatever that light is, it is not a star, Nancy thought. She was non-plussed and frightened by the sight. She grabbed the steering wheel and put the car back into gear quickly. Nancy eased the car back onto the road and jammed on the gas. She felt better when the strange light was behind her.

As Nancy drove on, she began to relax. Her mind was spinning with questions. What had she and Landy seen in the sky? How had it managed to change colors? What was it? She ran through the possibilities: airplane, tower lights, UFO, something else. Suddenly Nancy felt her stomach drop. Landy cried out, "Mom, there it is again."

Nancy stared in disbelief as the amber light once more appeared before them in the night sky. How had it gotten ahead of her? It had to be a plane of some sort or maybe even some type of satellite.

Nancy tried to calm down. She decided to take a photo of the light so she would have some proof of her story. Nancy began looking for a place to pull the car over again.

"Hold on, Landy. We're gonna get a picture of that funny light." Nancy tried to keep her voice calm.

She pulled off in a wide spot and put the car in park. Nancy had her camera in the car, as she often took photos of Landy when they went places. She retrieved the camera from the dash compartment and opened her car door to step out. The amber light hovered stationary in the night sky, and Nancy carefully framed the shot. She clicked off two quick shots and then paused.

The amber light quivered for a second and suddenly broke apart into two silver balls of light. Nancy would later tell investigators that the silver balls "began dancing around, one leaping in an arc over the other."

The silver balls shifted left and then shot away over the mountains. Nancy was suddenly alone with Landy on the dark, desolate road. She got back into her car and drove home. Later, Nancy would report her strange encounter to UFO investigators. Her photographs showed only a bright light in the sky. It was not something that investigators could work with. However, for Nancy and Landy, it was a singular experience that will remain with them forever.

What Flew Over Tyrone?

Dan Walton realized that he was going to have to hike off of Ice Mountain, near the city of Tyrone, after dark. It was October 20, 2002, and it had been a beautiful day for a hike. Dan had been so absorbed in the flora and fauna that he hadn't turned back early enough to be able to walk back to his car in the daylight.

Dan was making his way back to his car when he first noticed the bright light coming toward him from the north. Dan figured the object was an airplane. Suddenly, the light stopped in the sky and hovered. Much to Dan's shock, the light began to pulse. The light grew very dim before glowing bright again. As Dan watched, a reddish-orange halo began to encircle the object. Dan observed that the object was large and circular in form. However, the craft seemed to change to an egg shape as it began to pulse.

Dan could not believe what he was seeing. The lighted craft began to pulse faster and faster. Without warning, a very thin beam of brilliant, blue-white light shot from the bottom of the object toward the ground. Dan had never seen such a thing. It was not a normal searchlight, but instead more like the tight beam of a laser light. He guessed that the light was hitting the ground about a quarter mile away at a spot where a microwave relay tower blinked.

Dan was only about a hundred yards from his car, at which point he remembered that his camera was in the vehicle. Running forward, he unlocked the door and grabbed the camera. He brought it up and snapped a photo. The craft began to move in a tight circle and Dan snapped a second shot. He depressed the shutter a third time.

Suddenly the light shot upward at a tremendous speed and disappeared. Dan was left stunned and shaken. He would later tell researchers, "I don't know what this thing was, but I know I've never seen anything like it before." He told researchers that he hoped others would come forward and asked them to let him know if someone did, "If for no other reason, so I can stop questioning my sanity."

No one knows what flew over Tyrone that night, but whatever it was seems to have left Dan shaken and searching for a rational explanation.

GETTYSBURG UFO ENCOUNTER

Today Gettysburg is known for two things: the terrible battle fought there in 1863, and the ghosts that allegedly populate the town today. But Gettysburg also receives its share of UFO reports each year. In fact, there are some compelling UFO accounts from Adams and Franklin Counties in this book.

A person sent a story to www.ufovillage.com about a UFO encounter that occurred when his paranormal group visited Gettysburg. The gentleman stated that he and some friends were in Gettysburg in January of 2006. There was a mid-winter thaw and the group decided to go to the battlefield and do some ghost hunting.

The group met at Devil's Den and they were gratified to see that they were alone at the site. During the summer, Devil's Den is rarely a place where serious ghost hunting can be done. There are simply too many tourists there at that time of year, but in January it was perfect.

The group convened in the parking lot, talking about what they were going to do, when they caught a sudden glimpse of red above them in the sky. They looked up to see three red, spherical objects hovering above. The group watched transfixed as the objects moved from west to east over Little Round Top, where they lost sight of them. The group has no doubts that whatever they saw were large craft that moved silently across the night sky.

When the lights disappeared, the group began to discuss what they had just witnessed. No rational explanation was ever found for the three strange craft. Whatever they were, they certainly qualify as UFOs.

A Strange Development

Several years ago I was at a local eatery on the Broad Top in Bedford County. It was an old building with a ghostly tale and the owner came over to tell me the story. Another patron, a young man, heard the story and that I collected unusual tales. He introduced himself and told me that he had been a reporter for an area newspaper. He explained that he also had a strange story to tell.

"About two years ago I was given an assignment for the local paper. The railroad was going to tear down an old railroad bridge outside of Saxton. The bridge was a local fixture, an area where kids hung out to drink. They swam in the waters under the bridge, and more than one romance blossomed there. I was supposed to go out and take a final photograph for the paper. We were going to do a feature on it the following day.

"I had with me one of the cameras that the paper used. I was to just drop the camera off at the editor's office, and then go home. The feature was written already. It seemed like a very simple assignment.

"I drove out and walked way off so that I could get the bridge in completely. I adjusted the focus and snapped several shots. It was late in the afternoon and the light was perfect. I couldn't help but think that I had taken some great shots for the editor to choose from.

"I dropped off the camera just as I had been instructed to and went home. The next day I called the editor to ask him if the shots were okay. 'Do you mean the UFO shots?' he asked me.

"I had no idea what he was talking about but I soon found out.

"The editor had downloaded the camera and had noticed two large, circular disks above the bridge in the shots. They were in more than one shot and they were really quite big and clear. I'll never know why I didn't see them when I took the photos. Maybe it was just tunnel vision because I had a goal set in my mind.

"The editor had zoomed in on the shapes, and they definitely were two circular, disk-shaped craft in the sky. He ran the story along with a caption about UFOs visiting the Saxton area.

"I can't explain it, but the pictures clearly proved that something uncommon was in the sky that afternoon."

I thanked the fellow and finished up. It was a typical UFO story, and yet it was unique. I knew that one day I'd retell the reporter's story. Even when people are not looking for them, UFOs pop up in the strangest places.

HARRISBURG UFO

Mark put his signal on and eased the car onto Route 22 near Harrisburg. It was about 9 P.M. on a spring night in 1999 and he and his friend Ann were on their way to dinner. Mark was paying attention to the road as they headed into the city.

Ann was sitting in silence, looking out at the city lights and the other cars. Suddenly, she straightened up. "Look at that light up in the sky," she said, craning her neck to keep the light in view.

Mark snorted and kept on driving. It was a joke between him and Ann that she was always seeing strange lights in the sky and they always turned out to be explainable. Mark had laughed away more planes, satellites, and cell phone towers than he could possibly remember.

"Seriously," Ann insisted, "Look at that light. I've never seen anything like it."

Whatever the light was, it was staying ahead of them as the car traveled down Route 22. The fact that the light was keeping pace with the car eventually caused Mark to glance upward. He had to force his gaze back to the road. There was more than one light now, and they were keeping pace with the vehicle. Whatever the lights were, they were not airplanes or satellites.

Mark saw a restaurant ahead and eased the car off the road, quickly bringing it to a stop. He threw open the door and was out of the car within seconds. Ann also jumped out of the car and studied the sky.

Patrons coming and going were stopping to stare upward, too. Mark and Ann could hear people exclaiming as they pointed toward the sky.

Above in the night sky were three large white lights arranged in a row. Suddenly a fourth light flipped on. Then a fifth light flicked on.

Abruptly, one of the first three lights flipped off. Another light flipped off, and so it went. There seemed to be a maximum of five lights, but they continued to flip off and on in a random fashion. The white lights seemed to be on a large, dark craft, but it was difficult to make out the object because of the pulsing lights.

Mark picked up his phone and dialed a local radio station. He asked to speak to the newsroom but ended up with a deejay, who informed Mark that he was on the air. The deejay asked what news event he wanted to report. Mark explained that he was sitting in a parking lot watching what appeared to be a large lighted craft in the sky.

"A UFO," the deejay scoffed. "We have a fellow here who is seeing little green men!" She snorted in derision.

Mark was stung by the rude comments. The deejay was laughing at him. "What did you have for dinner?" the deejay demanded. "Must not have been legal!"

Mark hung up. Mark and Ann got back in the car and tuned the radio to the station that Mark had just called. Within seconds, another person came on air and announced that he was watching the lights, too. That was followed by another caller, and then another. Mark would later learn that people from all over the area were seeing and reporting the strange lights.

Mark and Ann listened as they resumed their journey. Within fifteen minutes, the deejay began reporting on the craft. "Folks, I have been told that the strange lights everyone is seeing in the sky are not from a plane at Fort Indiantown Gap on training exercises. Whatever you are all seeing, it isn't one of their craft."

Mark was not surprised by the announcement. He had already ruled out planes and helicopters. Whatever the thing was, it was much too large to be a helicopter. The object was hovering, so it could not be a normal plane. The craft was completely dark and very low, and it was perfectly noiseless. A helicopter could hover, but it could not do so soundlessly.

Another few minutes went by and the deejay was still reporting on the odd craft. It was evident that the deejay was not taking it seriously, and that was annoying Mark and many of the other listeners.

Suddenly the deejay announced, "Folks, I have just been informed that the craft that folks were seeing was only a helicopter from Fort

Indiantown Gap on maneuvers." Who did the deejay think she was fooling? Less than twenty minutes earlier she had said that the craft was not from Fort Indiantown Gap.

Within minutes, the lights from the craft all winked out. Then the lights came back on briefly before blinking out again. It was the last time that Mark and Ann would see the craft.

Mark was convinced that he had seen something that was not a regular aircraft of any kind. Mark would eventually write up an account of the events for a website. The site's hosts looked into the events and found that there was at least one more account of the same events reported to another website. What seems certain is that Mark and others did see something disturbing that night.

Lights over the Lake

Saylor's Lake is a private lake in Monroe County. The area is wildly rustic, and yet close to all the attractions of the Pocono Mountains. The lake is stocked with fish for the members to enjoy, and many of the houses there look out on the water. Lakeside cottages and substantial homes dot the wooded shoreline of the large lake. It is a private and quiet community, and certainly not a place where the state police have to patrol often. But on the night of March 1, 1973, the peace of Saylor's Lake was broken by a most unusual series of events.

At approximately 7:30 P.M. on that cold evening, several residents along the lake noticed odd lights over the water. Lights appeared in approximately fifteen-minute intervals and moved across the water from west to east before they disappeared. Sometimes a single white light danced across the lake, and at other times clusters of red, white, or blue lights flitted across the water at a height of approximately 1,500 feet.

The residents of the little waterside community were so concerned by what they were seeing that they called the state police. State trooper Jeffrey Hontz was sent to investigate the strange lights being reported by at least a dozen different residents. Trooper Hontz would later be quoted as saying that he saw four objects moving across the lake from west to east. "But don't ask me what they were," he said. "It was like Christmas trees flying in the air."

One area resident, Mrs. Pfeiffer, described the objects as being approximately the size of a child's wading pool. She stated that she and other residents counted at least thirty-nine objects moving across the sky over the lake. All together, the residents would report seeing forty-two bright flashing lights crossing the lake between 7:30 P.M. and 10:45 P.M. that night.

Skeptics claimed that what the residents witnessed were weather balloons, planes, or helicopters. All of the witnesses agreed that whatever they had seen, the objects were not conventional aircraft. They saw no sparks, they heard no noise, and they saw nothing to convince them that the light show came from any conventional source.

The Pymatuning Puzzle

Pymatuning State Park, in western Pennsylvania near the Ohio border, is a rugged and rustic area where a strange series of events supposedly unfolded on Labor Day weekend of 1988. According to the report, two couples were camping at Pymatuning Park for the holiday weekend. The two young couples had spent a typical day camping. They had made camp early in the day, gathered firewood for later that night, taken a hike, and just enjoyed some freedom in the great outdoors. They built a fire later in the evening and cooked supper over it.

Around 2 A.M., the couples were sitting and chatting quietly. Almost everyone around them had gone to sleep. The night sounds and the crackle of the fire punctuated their conversation. Everyone was feeling mellow as they enjoyed the night sky and bright stars.

The silence of the night was broken by a sound almost like a motor moving toward the campers. The sound was out of place in the woods and it attracted their attention quickly. The couples turned toward the lake, where the sound came from, and watched in shock.

Blue lights moving in a haphazard pattern swept across the lake. The couples stood up and watched in awe, barely believing their eyes. They had no context for what they were seeing. The lights shot across the lake repeatedly from one side to the other, then they all shot straight up in the air. Suddenly the lights all winked out. The entire display lasted approximately three minutes.

The couples discussed what they saw and they all agreed that they had seen the same thing. What that thing was, they didn't know.

Throughout the rest of their stay, they waited to hear someone else mention the strange lights, but no one did. Each night they sat up late waiting and listening in vain for the lights to return.

The couples ruled out aircraft, helicopters, spotlights, and other sources for the sounds and lights they saw that night. There are no cities near Pymatuning State Park and no airfields nearby, either. Neither couple had been drinking and they were all fully awake. The mystery of what they saw that night in the sky above Pymatuning Reservoir has remained for many years. The couples will most likely never know what they witnessed that warm summer night, but they all agree on what they saw and heard.

Close Encounters
of the First Kind

Historically, UFO sightings have been filed under several categories. The most common sightings are Close Encounters of the First Kind. These are defined as observing UFOs from a near vantage point (no more than five hundred feet). These encounters do not leave any trace in the local environment and there is no interaction with the human observer. No beings are seen during these encounters.

The Amazing Vanishing UFO

Bill Powell smiled at his passenger, Muriel McClave, and turned his attention back to the view through the front window of his personal plane. It was a beautiful afternoon in May 1966 and Bill was savoring this journey from Radnor to Philadelphia. He enjoyed the company of his friend, and he also loved to fly his plane, a silver Luscombe that he had been flying for years. Bill had logged 18,000 flight hours, many of them in his trusty Luscombe.

"We'll be passing over Willow Grove NAS," Bill informed Muriel. "Keep watching and you might see some military craft."

Muriel stopped her conversation and looked out the windows. Within seconds a squadron of Navy jets appeared, taking off from the base. Both Bill and Muriel watched in awe as each aircraft joined the formation and leveled off into its position. Bill was excited that his flight plan took them into such close proximity to the Navy jets.

Bill's eyes scanned the planes, and then he noticed something moving on the horizon. He expected it to be another plane, but that's not what he saw. A craft seemed to be following the Navy jets, but it couldn't be called a plane. It was a large, circular craft with a smaller bubble part on top. The circular-shaped section was bright red and the smaller portion was white, painted like a two-toned Cadillac. It was unlike anything Bill and Muriel had ever seen. The craft banked sharply away from the jets and headed directly for the Luscombe. Bill ran the angles in his mind and instantly realized that they were on a collision course. Making an evasive maneuver, Bill dodged the strange craft by less than one hundred yards.

When Bill turned the plane, he and Muriel got an up-close look at the odd craft. Bill observed that whatever it was, it was solid enough to block out the jets on the other side of it. He later estimated that the strange craft was traveling at about two hundred miles per hour.

As Bill turned his attention to maneuvering away from the craft, Muriel kept her eyes on it. She watched it slip past her window and she turned her head to follow it as it dropped slightly below and behind them.

With a shout of shock, Muriel twisted her head around both ways. The red and white craft had simply popped out of her sight. She could have sworn that it had just faded away.

Bill leveled off the plane and craned his neck to find the craft in case it had turned to try and strike them again. Muriel twisted around. "It's gone!" she cried out. "I saw it simply vanish."

She and Bill scanned the entire area looking for the craft, but it was no longer visible. Bill and Muriel would later report their encounter, and Muriel stated that she had been looking directly at the craft when it had disappeared.

Pilots are superb witnesses for UFO investigators to question. They are highly trained, analytical, and educated about flying. Bill, with his 18,000 flight hours, was an excellent witness, lending validity to his claim.

The Janesville Pike Incident

The evening of October 23, 1984, was cool and pleasant. M. L. Morrissey of Snyder Township, Blair County, was in his Ford pickup driving down the Janesville Pike, also known as Route 453. Morrissey was out spotlighting for deer, moving along at about forty-five miles per hour. The sky overhead was clear and he could not help glancing up every now and then to admire the beautiful starlit night.

At around 8:30 P.M., Morrissey slowed down to make a turn onto a winding old road. He looked up and, to his shock, saw a bright object approximately the size of a football field slip silently in front of him. Using a nearby set of power lines as a judge of distance and height, he estimated that the strange vehicle was moving along at forty miles per hour at an altitude of approximately one hundred feet.

Morrissey would later report that the object was mushroom-shaped and that it had dozens of red lights either blinking or rotating around the top of the craft. Along the stern, he saw six vertical panels of amber-colored light that stayed solidly lit.

In order to observe the craft better, Morrissey pulled off the road and turned off his vehicle. He wound down his window and listened intently, but he heard no engine sounds at all. He sat in his pickup truck and watched the mushroom-shaped craft for several minutes before it silently disappeared across the mountain ridge to the northeast of his position.

Morrissey would later contact UFO researchers in western Pennsylvania about his sighting. Dr. Paul Johnson and his team took the report, but they were unable to locate any other such encounters in the area of Snyder Township at or around the time Morrissey had his sighting.

Sky Witness

Jason sat back in his seat and relaxed as the airliner climbed to 22,000 feet, leaving the earth at Pittsburgh International Airport. Jason was on his way to Texas and was excited about the trip. He had managed to get a window seat, and he looked out at the amazing view of the city sprawled out below him. He always enjoyed viewing Pittsburgh this way.

It was 5 P.M. and the orange sky was brilliantly lit by the late-afternoon sun. Fluffy white clouds dotted the sky. Jason was enjoying the journey and wasn't anticipating any problems—but that was before he saw the first little black line streaking across the sky. Jason watched with idle curiosity as what appeared to be a black contrail formed in the orange sky. Looking for a source for the black vapor, Jason scanned the horizon. He followed the contrail outward but there was no vehicle at the lead end of it.

Jason watched in fascination as ten little black contrails suddenly appeared and joined up to create a straight line. The next moment, he caught sight of a new motion, and he observed a black circular craft hovering in the sky.

The contrails then split to create lines going in several directions. Jason watched the strange goings-on for nearly fifteen minutes before he saw the black craft suddenly zoom forward toward his plane. Red beams of light shot from the craft in the direction of the plane. For several seconds Jason feared that the craft was going to hit or shoot down the aircraft. He held his breath, waiting for the other passengers to call attention to the craft outside, but no one seemed to notice it. He wondered frantically if he was the only one looking out the window, but a quick glance around confirmed for him that others were also looking out the windows—and they didn't seem upset at all.

Jason bit his lip and waited. He expected the pilot to swerve, as the craft was in front of them and the pilot had to see it. The airliner didn't deviate at all, although Jason would later observe that the plane seemed to take a long time crossing the sky over Pittsburgh, based upon the length of time he witnessed the black contrails.

Finally, the plane passed by the black contrails and the black craft. No one else was reacting, so Jason sat still. He pondered what he had seen and tried to think of any rational explanation, but he could not come up with one. Jason would eventually tell his story on a website posting possible UFO experiences. Jason believes that he must have witnessed a UFO, and in the strictest sense of the term he did: He witnessed an unidentified flying object in the sky above Pittsburgh that afternoon, and it has left him questing for an answer ever since.

THE SHAPE~SHIFTING UFO

Joe and Jane Almond were on their way home after a pleasant evening out with friends. It was November 7, 2002, and they were not thinking about UFOs, but rather about the fun of the dinner they just had in Temple, Berks County. Joe was driving along Alsace Avenue and Jane was watching the houses as they passed. It was about 9:30 P.M. and the Almonds were not overly tired.

Suddenly Joe slowed the car down. He couldn't believe was he was seeing. Above a house ahead of them was a large object. It was cigar-shaped and was pulsing from a brilliant white to a faint glow.

"Stop the car," Jane cried. "Joe, stop!"

Joe put his signal on, despite the fact that no one was behind them, and he pulled over.

"Do you see that? What is it?" Jane's voice held awe, but Joe felt fear. He was wondering what it was, too.

As the couple watched, the object shifted shape and lengthened out. Then it shrunk again, and during that time it continued to pulse.

Joe felt compelled to open his car door and step out. He wanted an unobstructed view of the craft. A terrible, cold fear gripped Joe as he watched. Stepping forward to get closer, he suddenly felt strange. He wouldn't know until later, but in the car, Jane was suddenly feeling quite odd, too. The husband and wife were both feeling disoriented and disconnected, and they later said, "we suffered what seemed like an out-of-body experience, as though we ourselves were being uplifted into space."

Suddenly, the craft seemed to implode upon itself, and then it winked out. The Almonds were left shaken and disoriented. Joe and Jane made it home and talked about the experience. They eventually contacted the National UFO Reporting Center (NUFORC) and gave them a report of that night's events. Joe told them that he had drank a couple of cocktails earlier in the evening but his judgment was not impaired, while his wife had not had any alcoholic beverages. She also witnessed the same thing as he. The Almonds have no idea what they observed, but they do know that it was like nothing they had ever seen before.

Encounter in Washington County

It was a cool fall evening in 1998 and Ashley was hurrying to make it home after picking up her five-year-old daughter, Dana. It was already after 8 P.M. and she really needed to get home and make supper.

As Ashley drove along, she caught herself glancing up at the sky. There was something strange about it, she realized, so she slowed down and studied it. One of the stars was a different color. Ashley reached for her glasses as she studied the strange star. It was amber and was blinking slightly.

Ashley couldn't find her glasses, so she put on her signal to pull over when she came to a wide spot. She was on a rural road and there was little traffic.

Suddenly the object lit up and Ashley realized that she wasn't looking at a star; she was actually observing a craft. The object began to pulse red, blue, green, white, and back again. Abruptly the object shot backward and disappeared.

Ashley sat perplexed for a moment and looked over at Dana in her car seat. She was sleeping, and Ashley eased the car back onto the road.

Further down the road, the object reappeared. Ashley slowed down once more.

What was that thing? she wondered. She saw a wide spot ahead and pulled over once more. She had a small camera in the pocket of Dana's bag, so she dug into the bag and pulled the camera out. The light was amber once more and flashing as Ashley put the car in park and opened her door. She slipped out of the seat and stood up. As the light continued to flash, she began snapping shots of the craft so that she could show her husband later.

The light stopped pulsing and began to glow a steady amber. As Ashley watched in awe, the light suddenly split into two silver balls. The lights began to sway and hop back and forth. The one silver ball jumped over the other one, and the two lights shot off in different directions immediately after that.

Ashley jumped back into the car and quickly pulled out again. Her hands were shaking and her mind raced. Whatever the amber light was, it hadn't been earthly—of that she was sure.

THE STRANGE INCIDENT IN McKEAN COUNTY

Jason Hardcastle shuddered as he pushed open the door of his pickup truck. He had left his headlights on and the engine running. It was early December in 1982, and Jason was working for an oil company in McKean County, out in the woods between Bradford and the New York border. It was nearly midnight and the wind whipped and whistled around him. The snow picked up and swirled like grains of sand into Jason's face. He shivered and pulled his old work coat tighter around himself. He had to check to make sure that the equipment was working properly. There was some concern about the generator, and he had been volunteered for the duty of driving his four-wheel-drive pickup to the job site to check things out.

Jason noticed a bright light in the distance. The light was about 250 feet in the air and zigzagging downward toward him. As it dropped to 150 feet in altitude, the light was about 2,000 feet from him. Jason was bewildered as he observed it. It appeared to be a semicircle of light, and it began jumping to and fro again as it advanced on him.

The light continued moving until it was only about sixty feet from the truck and fifty feet up in the air. Jason stared in shock. He couldn't believe what he was seeing. A large circular craft hovered in the sky. It was lit and he could see it well. The craft seemed to be moving silently and there was no rush of air from it.

In the background, the generator droned on loudly. Suddenly the craft turned and a beam of light shot out of the ship directly at the generator, which instantly stopped working. Then the beam of light winked out and the generator buzzed back to life.

Jason bolted back into the truck. He was shaking with fear. What in the world was that thing? he wondered. He slammed the truck door and flipped his headlights off. He grabbed the gear shifter and rammed it back into reverse. Frantically, Jason turned and slid across the driveway. He had no idea what the craft at the oil rig site was or what the thing wanted, but he knew that he had to get away from it. He hoped that with the lights off, he wouldn't draw any attention and it would let him alone.

Suddenly the bright disc appeared in the sky above the moving truck. It had shot up to a height of nearly two thousand feet and was moving just ahead of the truck, keeping pace with it. Jason couldn't beat the craft, so he pulled over.

The craft hovered overhead and Jason sat there watching it. Suddenly the beam of light pierced the darkness again. Jason watched in awe and fear as the beam of light swept back and forth. Jason got the impression that the light was being used to search for something, but he had no idea what.

A second light beam appeared and Jason saw the circular craft that was emitting that beam. The second craft came in from the left side of the first craft, and the two ships seemed to be signaling each other using the light beams in flashing patterns. The second craft shot back the way it had come and disappeared from sight.

The first craft rapidly dropped until it was only about fifty or sixty feet in the air. Jason was paralyzed with fear as he watched the maneuver. Out of the blue, the truck radio began to blast static, despite the fact that the radio had not even been switched on. Jason dragged his eyes downward to watch the radio briefly.

Jason cried out as the truck began to rock back and forth, as if it was being shaken by a giant creature. Jason gripped the steering wheel and tried to see what was happening to the truck. A loud electrical humming filled the air, the truck radio burst with static, and Jason heard a loud crunching sound. He wasn't sure if the truck was being picked up or crushed.

Jason jammed the truck back into gear and was relieved to hear the tires bite into the gravel as he spun out. He drove frantically while he scoured the night sky for further sightings of the lighted craft, but he didn't see it.

Jason sped through the cold night to Bradford, where he pulled up at a friend's home. He got out and beat on the door until his friend Mark got up. Jason poured out his story and stood there shaking from cold and fright. Mark never even considered that Jason was playing a joke on him. Only one look at Jason's face convinced him that whatever had happened at the oil rig site, it had been terrifying.

Jason and Mark discussed it and Jason insisted that he wanted to take Mark back to the site to see for himself what had happened. Mark quickly dressed and jumped into the truck next to his buddy.

He didn't know what had happened in the woods, but he knew that Jason needed to go back and figure it out. Mark was sure that there had to be a logical explanation. Alien spaceships with light beams that shake trucks simply could not be real.

When the two men got to the oil rig, Jason parked the truck but left it running. Mark opened his door and felt the cold rush in. He scanned the night sky and his heart caught in his throat. In the distance he could see a large, lighted, round object. Mark stepped out of the truck to get a better look and Jason opened his door and stepped out, too.

"Now do you believe me?" Jason demanded. "There's something freaking strange up there. It's not like any plane I've ever seen."

Suddenly a loud electrical humming broke the silence of the night. Crunching sounds picked up as if a very heavy person was walking across the gravel toward them—but there was no one there. At that moment, both men dove back into the truck and Jason peeled out of the gravel driveway.

Neither man looked at the sky as they hurried out of the area. They were miles away before Jason slowed the truck down and they began to breathe easier. Neither one wanted to return to the site, and Mark was quite content to admit that Jason had not exaggerated or imagined his strange encounter.

The two men would later report their experiences to area UFO investigators. Much to their shock, they would learn that they were not the only ones to report strange encounters in the area that week. On December 8, three people from nearby Genesee observed a multi-colored craft over their home at about 7 P.M. In the Coudersport area, a man and his two children would also report seeing a strange craft just west of Route 6. They watched as the craft made a U-turn at an altitude of five hundred feet above their heads. The man would describe the craft as "stingray-like" and about seventy feet wide, but without a tail. The witnesses all agreed that the craft made a strange humming sound and it had red and white lights that were extremely bright. The lights were so bright that they obscured all other details of the vehicle. What was flying over the area that winter weekend? No one knows, but with so many witnesses who came forward, investigators are sure that something unusual was traversing the night skies of Bradford County.

Close Encounters of the Second Kind

C lose Encounters of the Second Kind are more disturbing. These sightings are at close range and leave some evidence. Evidence can be defined as broken branches, burned patches on the ground, animal disturbances, or malfunctioning of mechanical devices. Some people suffer physical effects, as well. These include, but are not limited to, sunburns, radiation poisoning, burning eyes, or physical illnesses. Those who have these encounters must also deal with the psychological damage that is left behind when their assurance of a normal, peaceful life is shattered.

The Mystery of the Disappearing Time

Ralph stepped outside and breathed in deep gulps of the fresh, cold night air in May 1973. He was a cook at a restaurant in the Oakland area of Pittsburgh. He wanted to clear his lungs of the fetid, damp air inside the restaurant and go home to his house on Squirrel Hill. Ralph was bone tired because he had worked sixteen hours that day. His legs were numb, and he knew that in the morning it would hurt to stand. He hadn't wanted the double shift, but a cook can't just leave the job unless there is someone there to take over for him.

Ralph shambled across the parking lot toward his Oldsmobile convertible and slid inside. He started the old car with a roar and pulled out into the early-morning traffic. Ralph nosed the car toward Schenley Park, which was the quickest way home.

As Ralph drove through Schenley Park, he suddenly felt an urge to pull over on the Oval in the park and take a nap. He just couldn't go any further. He had to rest.

Ralph pulled the car off the road and turned it off. He locked the doors and slid down in the seat so that he could sleep. He wished that he could have made it home, but suddenly his eyes felt leaden. He'd never been tired enough to pull over before, but on that night he just had to.

A bright shaft of white light startled Ralph and caused him to put his hand up to protect his eyes. He struggled awake, trying to understand what was going on. For a brief second he was confused, but then he remembered that he had pulled over to sleep. He tried to look past the bright beam to see the person who was holding the light. He half expected it to be a cop.

Ralph made out a figure in a blue-green metallic uniform, but he'd never seen such a uniform before. The bright light prevented him from seeing the person's face. All he could make out was an arm and a midriff. He shifted his gaze away from the painful light.

"What are you doing stopped here?" The figure's voice was low and definitely male. Ralph thought it was almost like it vibrated in his head.

"I stopped to get a little sleep. I was really beat from work." Ralph was still trying to determine if the fellow was a cop.

"What is sleep?" the figure asked. For a second Ralph was taken aback. He meant to answer, but he never had the chance.

When Ralph awoke again, he was in his own bedroom. He had no idea how he had gotten there. He clearly remembered stopping at the Oval to sleep. He remembered the figure with the bright light and the strange question, "What is sleep?"

Ralph looked at the clock and froze. He had lost more than twelve hours. It was now afternoon. He sat up and struggled to remember what had happened. He had to have driven home but he did not remember it. Ralph lived with his parents, and he would later ask them if they had heard him coming in that night. It had been so late that they had been in bed and couldn't remember him arriving home.

Throughout the following days, Ralph developed a terrible rash across his groin. He also developed the same rash across his hairline. Then a group of warts developed in the rash on his groin. Ralph treated the rash and it eventually disappeared, but the warts remained. He sought medical help, but the doctors couldn't explain the sudden development of the warts. The rash would reoccur for many years and Ralph would suffer from painfully sensitive skin across his groin.

Eventually Ralph's story reached the ears of a UFO researcher who contacted him about it. Ralph patiently answered the questions presented by the researcher. The researcher questioned him about the man with the bright light. Ralph recalled that the man was average in every way, but he did remember that the man had some sort of patch or insignia on his uniform. He couldn't draw the symbol, though.

Ralph would not agree to be hypnotized in order to recall more details. The researchers did consider the possibility that the man with the bright light was a park policeman, but their uniforms were not metallic.

When Ralph's case was presented in the January 1983 issue of *PCUFOR Researcher*, Dr. Paul Johnson did not conclusively rule it a UFO encounter. He related it and allowed the reader to keep an open mind. As for Ralph, he felt that whatever had happened to him was not natural, and it left him very unsettled.

THE MYSTERIOUS CASE OF THE UNUSUAL CRAFT

For sixteen-year-old Ross Guidotti, Saturday nights were usually a time when he could hang out with his friends, but on the night of February 26, 1983, Ross was babysitting his little sister, Katie. It was not what he would have chosen to do, but his folks had asked him to babysit so that they could go out, and he had little choice but to comply. At least Ross had phone privileges and he was currently talking to his friend David Witmer while his sister played.

Ross didn't expect anything exciting to happen that night in the Pittsburgh suburbs, but that was before he looked out the window. Ross was still chatting to David on the phone when he first noticed the bright dot of light in the sky. As he watched it curiously, he wondered what it was that could move so rapidly and at such odd angles.

Ross stopped paying attention to the telephone call. The light was getting bigger and moving from the north toward his house at a rapid speed. It looked huge now and was brightly lit. Fear swelled in Ross's throat. Was that an airplane? Was it going to crash into his house? It seemed to be coming directly at him, and whatever type of plane it was, it was round and about a hundred feet wide!

"Something's coming toward my house," Ross cried out to his friend on the phone. "I've got to go . . . "

He hung up the phone, and that was when his dog, Aero, caught his attention. The dog was backed up into a corner and was whimpering and whining as he stared at the light, too.

The lights in the living room began to blink as if there was some sort of electrical interference. Katie began crying. Ross stared around at the pulsing lights, and then glanced out the window. None of the other houses seemed to be having electrical trouble. Was the lighted craft causing it?

The craft's lights were so bright that they nearly blinded Ross as he tried to make out the shape of the object. He expected to hear a sound, but there was total silence from the craft, which was now above the house. He strained to hear motor noises but all he heard was the dog whimpering, Katie crying, and his own pounding heartbeat.

As Ross looked out the window, the large ship crossed over his home. He estimated that the craft was about eighty feet in the air and he could make out the rounded front edge of the object, but the back edge was blurred by the light.

The craft shot upward and was gone. Ross scanned the darkness for some indication that the ship was returning, but there was no sign of it now. Ross tried to calm Katie, who was now clinging to him, asking if the bright light was over and if it was going to hurt them.

Beside the phone was a list of emergency telephone numbers that Ross's mother always left when they went out. Their next-door neighbor was at the top of the list. With shaking fingers, Ross dialed Cindi Siwick's number. He told her what had happened and she said that she'd be right over.

When Cindy got to the house only moments later, she asked Ross to step outside. The two stood in the front yard scanning the sky. Suddenly Ross saw a pinpoint of light moving much like the mysterious craft had been earlier. He pointed it out and they both watched as the bright white light came toward them from a southerly direction.

As the two stood watching, the light rapidly moved closer. They could see that it was circular and bright white. The light appeared several times bigger than the stars, and it began to dance around. First it moved back and forth, and then from side to side. That was when the lights began to pulse in different colors. The craft finally settled on a red pattern.

Whatever the object was, Ross knew enough to recognize that it wasn't a conventional aircraft. First of all, the shape was all wrong and it moved in ways that no normal plane could. He would later estimate that he and Cindi watched the craft for nearly twenty minutes.

Cindi finally tired of watching the light and informed Ross that she was going down to the local convenience store for something. Whatever the light was, it was far enough away that it couldn't hurt them. She brushed off the sighting and hurried to run her errand.

Ross was still rattled and he felt that he needed to let someone know about what he had seen. Every cheesy old sci-fi movie he had ever watched jumbled through his head and he knew that he had to call the police.

Ross called the South Park police station and poured out his story of the strange light that jumped around in the sky and changed colors. An officer on the other end said that a car would be sent out there, but he cautioned Ross that this had better not be a joke or prank.

Ross returned to watching the light but was disappointed when it began to fade from view about half an hour later. The police had not yet arrived. When they did come, they doubted Ross's story because the light was gone.

Cindi, however, would be the one to confirm Ross's strange tale. After she left Ross, she had gone to the convenience store. She would later tell investigators that she had seen two small lights low to the ground. A beam of light shot up from the ground into the sky. She would later say, "It was like nothing I ever saw."

Meanwhile, Ross had been outside scanning the sky for the lights he had seen before the police arrived. The police left, and Ross continued his vigil. He finally checked the sky one last time and then turned to go back into his house. It was getting late and he was tired and shaken. Suddenly he stopped and stood very still. He saw what he later described as "two dinner plate-shaped craft" above and behind the last house on the block. He reported that one plate-shaped craft was upright while the other was upside down on top of it. The two "plates" made up two parts of a larger craft, and the edges of the ship were brightly lit. Ross tore his eyes away from the craft to scan the sky for any other objects, and in that instant the lighted ship blinked out or disappeared.

Ross would later call the *Pittsburgh Press* newspaper to inquire about other possible UFO sightings. He would tell reporter Don Hopey that he had also contacted Buhl Planetarium and had asked if they had received any other sightings. Ross said that the planetarium had told him that they had fielded three other calls about possible sightings in the same area where Ross had his encounter.

Don Hopey contacted UFO researcher Diane Enion, whom he had worked with on earlier UFO sighting cases. Enion found in her research that the planetarium did not keep a registry of UFO reports, but they did confirm that they had received three other reports the night of Ross's encounter. Diane Enion and the PCUFOR team could not find any other persons willing to admit that they had experienced anything unusual on the night in question in the South Park area. Furthermore, no one contacted the *Pittsburgh Press* after Hopey ran a story about the UFO sighting on Thursday, March 3, 1983.

Ross Guidotti and Cindi Siwick would be left with no explanation for what they had encountered on that cold winter's night. What type of craft appears as "two dinner plates" upside down on each other? And what about the strange lights that had plagued them that night? All that the two were left with were questions—questions that would never be answered.

ANGEL HAIR

One of the problems with UFO encounters is that they are usually based solely upon eyewitness accounts. However, there are some encounters that do leave evidence. One type of evidence is "angel hair." Angel hair is a mass of cobwebs or jelly-like substances associated with UFO sightings. Quite often the angel hair evaporates shortly after the sighting. Some researchers speculate that angel hair is formed by ionized particles, which are created by the electromagnetic fields believed to be around UFOs.

It was about 2 P.M. on May 4, 1981, when Bill Hummer backed his motorcycle out of the driveway of his home in Danville. As Bill was about to leave his driveway, he paused. There were masses of cobweb-like material everywhere. He saw the cobwebs hanging off the telephone lines, spread over the houses, and draped across the parked cars. He dismounted and reached out to touch some of it, but it melted away under his fingertips. Looking up he thought he glimpsed motion in the sky near the sun.

In order to see better, Bill ran inside and got his binoculars. Back outside, he focused them on the area where he had detected motion. He saw the motion again and focused in. There were discs moving up there. He later described them as "these things—discs—working back and forth, and this stuff was coming down continuously."

At that moment, a deliveryman stopped in front of Bill's house with a package. He got out of the truck and looked around, stunned. The man reached out to pick up some of the angel hair off of a car, but it evaporated as soon as his skin touched it. Bill pointed upward and the two men began to watch the activity in the sky. At length, one of the crafts shifted position so that it was away from the sun. Bill later described it thus: "It was round and metal with a dome and a kind of peak on it. It flew off one way and tilted down, and I got it good in the binoculars."

For half an hour the two men watched the craft working and the masses of angel hair continued to fall. Bill's sister, Marie, pulled in to visit their mother, who lived with Bill. She was also shocked by what she was seeing and joined the men in watching the UFOs in the sky making masses of angel hair.

Bill managed to get a handful of the material, but as he crunched it in his palm, it disappeared. It was white and almost ash-like. None of them had ever seen anything like it. Bill would report the angel hair to the police and eventually UFO researchers were called in. Many people saw the angel hair, and several were interviewed by researchers. No conventional explanation was ever found for the strange cobwebs that covered the Danville neighborhood.

WHAT DIANE SAW

Seventeen-year-old Diane watched the highway as she came home from work one night in 1967. She was driving her parents' 1954 Chevy, heading east about three miles outside of the little town of Gettysburg. She turned onto Hunterstown Road, in an area where there were several small power plants scattered over the terrain. That's when she first saw it: a large, saucer-shaped craft hovering above one of the power plants. Diane put on the brakes and slowed to observe the object.

The next thing she knew, the craft was just above her car and keeping pace with her. She was still on the road and driving as if she hadn't slowed down. The craft could not have been more than a hundred feet above the car and was keeping pace with it. From such close range, Diane could see the object well. The craft was metallic in appearance. It glowed brightly and she could see windows all around the side of the craft. She did not see any movement, but she could see that the craft was larger than her car and was capable of holding several figures. It made no sound. She knew immediately what she was seeing, for there had been a rash of UFO sightings in the Gettysburg area that summer. Her heart beat loudly and she hurried toward her home and safety.

Diane could not go fast on the twisting back roads, so she had plenty of time to observe the craft. It did nothing aggressive, but she could not shake it. Finally her house came in sight, and she swung the Chevy into the driveway and pulled up beside the house. To her surprise, the saucer stopped above the road and hovered there. It didn't make the turn. It dawned on her that the craft had only moved in a straight line from the power plant as she drove along the road.

Diane threw open the car door and ran into the house. She poured her story out to her mom and the two women went back outside. To Diane's relief the saucer was still there, hovering about 150 feet above the road. Diane and her mother watched the object for nearly fifteen minutes. No other traffic came along the road during that time.

Pictures! Diane ran inside for the camera, but it had no film. She wouldn't be able to get photos of the craft.

Diane and her mother went back inside and her mother called the local radio station. They spoke to the newsroom and were told that there had been many sightings of a craft or a large light in the sky that night. They gave a report of their sighting and hung up.

Now that Diane was home she had calmed down considerably. She went back inside and called a girlfriend and told her what was outside. The friend didn't immediately believe her but said that she'd try to get over as soon as possible.

Finally, Diane's mother told her that they needed to get Diane's sister. The craft had not done anything aggressive, so Diane and her mother decided that Diane could leave the house to go down the road a few miles and get her sister.

Diane backed the car out and nosed it back onto the road. The craft lurched forward and took up its position above her car. It followed her until she turned off on a side road. Diane could see the craft hovering above the ground as if waiting for her to return. She again puzzled over the idea that the craft was only moving in a straight line from the power plant.

Diane pulled up in front of where her sister worked and her younger sister ran over and got into the car. Diane told her what had been happening that night. Her sister was shocked and upset. She shuddered and averred that she didn't want to see the UFO. By now Diane had adjusted to the situation. She was more excited than upset by the sightings. Nothing interesting ever happened in Gettysburg, but this was very cool!

Suddenly the craft, or another just like it, was off to her left above another of the little power plants as she drove by it. She called out to her sister to look but her sister hid her head instead. The craft took up position above her and moved along for a couple minutes. Suddenly it vanished and then reappeared above her car again a moment later. It followed her toward another power plant she had to drive by, and then it was gone.

Diane's sister has stoutly maintained that she never saw the craft because she refused to look. Diane's mother will vaguely mutter that "there was something strange that night but I don't know what." Diane, however, is very clear that she saw a saucer-shaped UFO above the power plant and that it followed her home. She further saw it or one like it above two other little power plants along her path. Diane does not believe that she was abducted, despite her inability to remember what happened between seeing the craft over the power plant and the moment when it began to hover over her car.

There were so many sightings in Gettysburg that year that the children in school began drawing and painting UFOs for art class. Diane stated that she remembered going to school and seeing hallways filled with such artwork, and many of the renderings bore a striking resemblance to what had followed her that night.

THE BELLWOOD HORROR

On October 15, 1983, sixty-seven-year-old housewife Catherine Burk was driving along Route 220 near Bellwood. It was about 8:30 P.M. and night had fallen. The lights of Burk's 1976 Chevy Malibu cut through the darkness as she drove.

Catherine heard a loud whirring noise. As she braked, trying to figure out where the sound was coming from, she saw a large light coming in her direction. A large, silver, disc-shaped UFO appeared in her line of vision. She was shocked to see the twenty-four-foot-wide disc heading for her only about thirty feet off the ground. The strange craft rushed at her and she was sure they would collide. She felt the left side of her car lift off the road. Panic grabbed Catherine. She couldn't steer the car. For approximately five seconds the car's left side was about three feet off the ground. She screamed as the car fell back to the ground with a grinding thud. Catherine was badly jarred, having been knocked into the dash and jolted around inside the car.

She struggled to steer the car but it wasn't responding, and the steering wheel was difficult to turn. Catherine tried to get the vehicle off the road, but the car had stalled. She was frantic to get it going. The UFO was still in the area, she just knew it. She turned the ignition but the car refused to start. Again and again she tried to get the car started, but nothing worked. Catherine was crying, and she gripped the steering wheel and tried to calm down.

The craft was gone and Catherine needed to get her wits about her. She had to get the car going, but she thought she may have flooded the engine. Catherine forced herself to calm down and wait to try and start it again. It was nearly half an hour until the car sputtered, and then roared choppily to life. The engine didn't sound right and it choked, almost dying, but she pulled the knob to turn the lights on and nosed the car back onto the road.

The journey home was less than pleasant. Several times the car sputtered to a stop and Catherine had to try and remain calm. She wanted to hurry but she wasn't sure that it would do her any good.

The woman nearly sobbed when she finally saw her home approaching. She got out of the car and ran for the house. She turned and glanced up at the sky before slamming the door. She hadn't seen anything.

Burk made it as far as her kitchen chair before she began to cry. Her family came running and tried to comfort her. Her story was incredible, but they had only to look at her face to know that she was telling them the truth.

The Bellwood police were called but were unable to find anything that either substantiated or disproved the story. The Bellwood police chief at the time, Gregory Ciaccio, would assert in a later interview that he found Burk badly shaken and that she "was not drinking. The witness appeared to me to be sincere and honest, and not one to concoct a story such as this."

Mrs. Burk was taken to Mercy Hospital, where she was treated for several injuries. She had a bruised shoulder, spinal problems, bruises on her chest, and possible cracked ribs, and she had lost the hearing in her right ear. Her injuries required that she wear a neck brace. She had obviously been through severe physical trauma.

It was the Bellwood police who reported her case to the UFO Hotline. MUFON (Mutual UFO Network) was notified and sent researcher Scott Crain Jr. of Port Matilda to investigate. Crain's investigation came up with three other people in Blair County who reported seeing something odd in the sky that night.

Mrs. Burk seemed to suffer some lasting physical effects from her encounter, including difficulty hearing out of her right ear for some time after the strange incident. She also experienced symptoms related to post-traumatic stress.

In a strange postscript, the morning after Mrs. Burk's harrowing experience, she looked out her window and was shocked to see some strangely dressed men measuring her car. The men moved stiffly, were dressed in black suits, and were very formal. She hurried outside and demanded to know what they were doing. The men ignored her and continued to work. Mrs. Burk grew upset and insisted that they leave. The men eyed her dispassionately and simply walked away. Only later would she learn about "the men in black." The men she described were similar to the classic figures of UFO lore.

A UFO Named Floyd

April 17, 1966, began as a normal Sunday for Portage County (Ohio) sheriff's deputies Dale Spaur and Wilber "Barney" Neff. They were on patrol in the early-morning hours when they first saw what looked like an abandoned car pulled off to the side of Route 224 not far from Ravenna, Ohio. The two officers pulled over and got out to check the vehicle.

To their surprise, the car was filled with electrical equipment. It was very odd to see an abandoned car filled with high-tech gadgets. Furthermore, the car had a strange insignia on the side doors. There was a triangle and the words, "The Seven Steps to Hell."

The two officers were pacing around the car trying to figure out what they were dealing with when they first spotted the bright light. It rose above the treetops on a nearby hill and they stared at the object in awe. They'd never seen anything quite like it. The object was shaped roughly like a football and the steady light came from the bottom of it. The light was so bright that it hurt to look at it, and the officers had to avert their eyes.

The object shot forward until it was hovering over them. The officers were gripped by fear. They needed help. Spaur would later say, "I was petrified, and so I moved my right foot, and everything seemed to work all right. And evidently he [Neff] made the same decision I did, to get something between me and it. So we both went for the car, we got in the car and we sat there." Neff was behind the wheel and Spaur grabbed the radio. They told the dispatch officer, a Sergeant Schoenfelt, that they were observing a disc-shaped craft approximately 40 feet in diameter and about 250 feet away from them. In the backs of their minds was the memory that the day before a terrified woman had reported a UFO sighting. Everyone had laughed at her, but Neff and Spaur weren't laughing now.

The dispatcher came back at Neff and Spaur and instructed them to keep the craft in sight. He was hoping to get a photographer to the scene.

Suddenly the UFO shot forward and the officers gave pursuit. Spaur manned the radio while Neff drove. Spaur gave their position and informed dispatch that they were traveling at speeds in excess of one hundred miles per hour. He asked for further direction.

When the UFO shot too far ahead, it paused to wait for them to catch up. It was as though the craft was playing tag with them.

Police Chief Gerald Buchart of Mantua, Ohio, was contacted and he realized that the officers and the UFO would be passing his house. He grabbed a camera and ran outside. To his shock, the reports were true. He had never seen anything like the craft. He managed to snap two poor-quality photographs of the UFO.

Police officers along the way began to radio what they were observing as the strange chase progressed. Police Officer Wayne Huston of East Palestine, Ohio, a town just beyond the Pennsylvania border, informed dispatch that he was en route and would be intercepting Spaur and Neff's car.

Huston picked up the chase and slipped into place behind the first police car. The UFO was headed east along Route 224 into Pennsylvania. The officers radioed ahead to let the Pennsylvania State Police know what was coming their way. The chase had been uneventful so far in part because it had occurred so early in the day. There was little traffic to contend with. The UFO would repeatedly slow down or loop back to make sure that the police officers were still following it.

As the first light of morning lit the sky, the officers got their first good look at the craft. They realized that the entire craft had not been illuminated. The craft was roughly saucer shaped but behind it was a metal tail that had not been lit.

The strange procession made its way toward the little town of Conway, Pennsylvania. Neff and Spaur had been chasing the UFO for over an hour by now. They were tired, shaken, and running low on fuel. They ran up the main drag of Conway and saw a police car sitting along the road. They explained that they were nearly out of gas and requested that the officer, patrolman Frank Panzenella, pick up the chase.

The police cars pulled over, and the UFO stopped and seemed willing to wait. Panzenella got out of his car and stood with the other officers watching the strange disc.

Panzenella radioed in to his dispatcher with information about what he and the other officers observed. The dispatcher then contacted radar technician William Akers at the Greater Pittsburgh Airport tower. He explained what was happening and asked if there was anything strange on the radar. Akers responded that he saw nothing on the radar.

The Air Force had also been notified, and within minutes the four officers on the ground saw military fighter planes appear in the sky. As soon as the fighters appeared, the UFO shot upward rapidly. The UFO had been hovering between one hundred and two hundred feet in the air until that point, hugging the trees and mountaintops. It backed off considerably, and then suddenly the craft simply vanished. The officers would insist that it hadn't just gone so high they could not see it. The craft had been visible until it suddenly accelerated and vanished.

Project Blue Book was an Air Force program designed to look into possible UFO sightings at that time. It was run by Major Hector Quintanilla, who was contacted and rapidly assembled the police officers involved. Within hours Quintanilla had questioned the four men. Spaur would later state that Quintanilla had been determined to explain away the sighting no matter what the officers said. He began his questioning of Spaur by saying, "Tell me about this mirage you saw."

The police officers were told that they had all been chasing a mirage. They were instructed to sign a statement that said that the sighting had lasted for mere moments. The officers argued that the statement was filled with lies. They had clearly seen a craft of some sort, and not a "mirage." Spaur and Neff asserted that they had chased the object for more than an hour. They did not want to lie.

As soon as Quintanilla realized that the officers were not going to acquiesce, he ended the questioning. Spaur would later testify that the entire questioning session he had with Quintanilla had lasted perhaps two and a half minutes. Quintanilla then informed them that the official verdict would be that the event was really "an astronomical phenomenon." The official statement would indicate that Spaur and Neff had first seen a satellite and then had given chase to the planet Venus.

Mantua police chief Buchart backed up the police officers from both Ohio and Pennsylvania. He came forward to indicate that he and his wife had both seen the craft from their front yard, and that they had taken photographs of the object shortly after the chase had begun. He showed the photographs to the *Cleveland Plain Dealer*, but later refused to allow the shots to be published. He told the reporter that he had been instructed by the Air Force not to publish them.

A week after Deputy Spaur first saw the craft, he spotted it again. This time the police officers decided to name the craft "Floyd" so that those monitoring the police band would not know what they were talking about.

For the four officers who chased the UFO, life would change drastically. They all took a great deal of razzing about the events. Some of them lost their jobs or saw their marriages fall apart. Deputy Spaur watched his entire life unravel, and he and his wife divorced. His ex-wife would later state that he was never the same after that UFO chase. He claimed to see the UFO a couple more times, and he could not handle the stress that it put on his life.

There is no more compelling case in the annals of American ufology than this multistate chase. This case actually inspired the chase scene in the movie *Close Encounters of the Third Kind*. In total, nearly a dozen highly trained police officers from both Pennsylvania and Ohio observed something that they steadfastly refused to believe was a satellite or the planet Venus. The officers refused to recant their stories, and would later testify to the National Investigations Committee on Aerial Phenomena (NICAP) about their experiences. The information, signed statements, tapes, and sketches were compiled into an exhaustive report that was delivered to congressional investigators. It was also hand delivered to the University of Colorado UFO Project initiated by the government in 1966. The subsequent report put together by Dr. Edward U. Condon, known today as the Condon Report, would not even mention this fantastic case. One is left to wonder why.

THE CARBONDALE MYSTERY

November 9, 1974, marks the date of one of the strangest and most controversial stories in Pennsylvania ufology. That was the night when the Carbondale mystery began.

Three teenage boys—fifteen-year-old Bill Lloyd, his fourteen-year-old brother John, and their friend, fifteen-year-old Bob Gillette Jr.—were all hanging out in the small town of Carbondale on that Saturday evening. It was about 7 P.M. when they saw a bright object streaking across the sky. It was golden white and it came from the direction of Salem Mountain outside of town.

The boys figured from the trajectory that the object had come down near Russell Park somewhere between the town cemetery and a pond. The boys headed to the area and looked around. They found a four-foot-wide glowing spot in an old mine silt pond. They'd later describe it as lit with a bright yellow pulsing glow that had a red core. Because of the silt, sulfur and other mining contaminants, the water was green and the yellow light highlighted that, giving the water an eerie green glow.

The boys went to summon help. They didn't know what had fallen in the pond. It could have been a meteorite or anything.

The first people that they told about the strange light were three friends. Armed with reinforcements, the six boys went back to check it out again. Gillette and the Lloyd boys swore that the light had changed position in the water. It was now about twenty feet out in the deeper water.

The boys went home and told their parents, who in turn called the police. The police did not immediately respond, and they were called twice before anyone bothered to check it out. Two Carbondale police officers—a Patrolman Barbero and an Officer Jacobina—met the boys at the scene. By now it was nearly 10 P.M. They could clearly see the glow beneath the surface. The two officers discharged their revolvers into the water at the glowing object and it moved away from the shots. That was enough to convince them that something mysterious was going on. Another police cruiser was called, and an Officer Eltrilla joined the scene.

The boys would later tell the *Carbondale News* that the Mitchell Hose Company emergency truck was sent for, along with a boat. Portable lights were set up at the edge of the water and the police made plans to retrieve the object. They boys saw a photographer taking dozens of photos of the glowing object and the scene. Officer Eltrilla got in the boat and tried to touch, move, or scoop up the object with a large net.

Eltrilla would be quoted as saying, "Three witnesses reported to us that the UFO . . . landed in the middle of this pond, then proceeded under the water to approximately 25 feet from the shore."

The boys said that as they stood near the police car where they had been told to stay, a voice came over the radio instructing the officers to "hold off the news media." They would later claim that the police told them that the object was a meteorite.

By now the parents of the boys were getting concerned. What had their children gotten involved in? Bob Gillette's grandfather tried to find out what was happening and was told that the boys were "working" in Russell Park. By the time that the boys returned home it was after 1 A.M. The mysterious light would glow for nine hours after its discovery by the boys.

The following day, the boys could not contain their curiosity and they returned to the park to see what had happened. They were surprised to find that they were not allowed in the area. Acting police chief Francis Dottle was prohibiting people from entering the pond area. The boys saw a crane being taken to the area; they waited for a long time, but it never returned. They later speculated that it must have left by another path or road. Perhaps the oddest thing that the boys saw while loitering in the area all afternoon was a local delivery truck going down the path to the pond. They wondered why on earth a delivery truck was going down there.

The boys found a vantage point where they could see the operations in the pond. There were many other curious onlookers as well. In fact, photographs from the time show people ringing the hill above the pond, and even a group of children sitting in an abandoned coal chute watching the officers working. The boys later told reporters that at some point before the delivery truck arrived, a scuba diver entered the water. He returned a bit later visibly shaken and gesturing wildly with his arms. It appeared to the boys that the police officers tried to calm and quiet the diver.

The following day the boys once again returned to the pond. This time the atmosphere was vastly different from Sunday. On Monday the press was welcomed and encouraged to attend. The general public was also allowed to go into the area once more. As everyone watched, a police diver went into the water and came out about ten minutes later carrying a railroader's lantern.

The mystery was solved and most of the town went home satisfied. It was a hoax, everyone said, and the boys were the prime suspects. The boys later granted an interview to local media in which they defended themselves. They told their story of the secret doings on Sunday. The boys claimed that the police had put the lantern there to make them look like fools and to protect the secret of what the police had really taken from the water on Sunday.

So what fell into the pond at Russell Park that day? Through the years, there has been a great deal of speculation about the events. Was it a meteorite? If so, why would the police want to keep it a secret?

Bits and pieces of information released in the ensuing years create another scenario. Robert D. Barry, the director of the Twentieth Century U.F.O. Bureau of Collingswood, New Jersey, unearthed another story that might explain the questionable actions of the local police.

According to Barry, what really happened that night was that Soviet satellite Luna 23 crashed into the pond. Using information from articles that appeared in *TASS*, the publication of the Soviet news agency, and documents and interviews with military personnel, he theorized that Luna 23 crashed into either the pond or nearby Elk Lake.

Barry interviewed many of the key players and made some interesting discoveries. He states that he and an associate examined two strips of 35mm film with photos of the light in the pond. He requested copies of at least two frames from the police in possession of the film but was denied. He also interviewed the officers there and learned that the object was apparently very hot, because it hissed at times as if it was emitting steam. Officer Eltrilla stated that the glowing area was approximately twenty feet in circumference.

Barry also states in his report that not only had the three boys seen the object streak across the sky before it fell into the pond, but several adults had, too. This became very important later on.

In 1999, on the twenty-fifth anniversary of the event, Bob Gillette Jr. would change the debate substantially. He announced in the November 7 *Scranton Sunday Times* that the entire thing was a hoax. According to thirty-nine-year-old Gillette, he had thrown a flashlight into the silt pond that day to frighten his sister, Maria, and her friends. He said that before they could get his sister and her friends to the scene, the light burned out. The teens then stole a lantern from a parked car and lit it. That was the lantern that the police retrieved.

So what is the truth? Did a UFO crash in the silt pond? Did a Soviet satellite drop there or in Elk Lake on that night? Did teenage boys play a spectacular prank that has entered the annals of UFO lore? The truth may never be known. As time goes by, stories change and memories shift. Today it is up to the reader to decide. However, no look into Pennsylvania's dark UFO history would be complete without a visit to Carbondale and the old mining silt pond where lore, legend, and hoax may well have mixed to create a tale that will long be told.

Something Strange Along the Road

The stretch of highway between Penn and Manor, east of Pittsburgh, is not particularly special in any way. People drive through every day and don't think anything about it. But during the night of April 15, 1973, many of those who drove along that stretch of road had cause to long remember what happened to them.

That evening, more than a dozen different people reported seeing a large disc-shaped object in the sky along that stretch of highway. It was reported that the disc was metallic in appearance, and estimates of its size ranged from 35 to 60 feet. The reports estimated that the craft came within 200 to 250 feet of the observers. Many of the observers reported that the headlights of their cars dimmed or blinked off and on as if there was a power drain or electrical disturbance.

Near Jeanette, an observer noticed a large glowing craft hovering over the railroad tracks in the area of a power plant. The craft was approximately forty feet long, and it seemed to be completely solid with a dome-shaped top. It was nearly 11 P.M., but the witness reported that the object lit up the entire area with a brilliant white light. The witness could clearly see the trees and the scenery. The white light was so bright that it was painful to look directly at it. The craft had three rows of multicolored lights and the witness could see square portholes or windows spanning the length of it. The windows alternated in color. They ran green, blue, and red in a repeating pattern.

The witness pulled over the car and got out. The headlights of the car dimmed as he watched the craft in awe. It was no more than a hundred feet away from the man and only about four hundred yards away from the power plant. The craft skimmed barely ten feet above the trees, making the treetops sway and bend.

A long, glowing rope or tube of sorts hung from the side of the craft; at the end of it was a human-shaped figure. The witness stated that the being had to be ten feet tall. It moved much like astronauts did in space. The being glowed a strange red/purple color. As the witness watched, the glowing cord blinked out and the figure disappeared. The witness noticed a thin, high, whining noise, "like a spinning top," just before the craft quickly winked out and disappeared.

MICHELE'S STORY

Michele is a vivacious woman who enjoys life and all that it has to offer. You have only to speak to her for a few moments to realize that she's extremely intelligent and well grounded. She is a retired schoolteacher who took up a second career as a jewelry maker for a store in western Pennsylvania.

Approximately a decade ago Michele began to suffer strange nightmares. In her dreams, she was often in a school with other people who were learning from an oddly shaped alien being. The creature unnerved her. Other dreams were even stranger and darker. She dreamed that some creature was observing as she and her husband were intimate. It was shameful, but somehow she always felt distant from the events.

Michele was a voracious reader, and when someone mentioned to her that they had read of similar dreams in books on alien abductions, she was intrigued. The concept stirred something in her memory. She read book after book on the subject, but they offered her no help. But then she read a book by an author who claimed that aliens were marking their victims with luminous goop that would only show up under black lights. He explained that not all black lights are the same; it had to be a specific type of black light that was used by jewelers looking for flaws in gems.

Michele read the information with interest. She worked for a jewelry store and had exactly the type of black light that was mentioned in the book. She felt ashamed of herself, but she ran it over her body one morning after a shower. Nothing. But the book did say that the markings faded with time.

What Michele was thinking was incredible to her. She could not voice her thoughts to anyone else. She decided that she'd wait until there was another dream and then try the light again. If there were no markings at that time, then she'd admit that her idea was foolish. However, Michele almost felt compelled to give the theory a try. She felt deep within herself that what the book described had been happening to her, but she didn't know why she had this conviction. She had only the dreams and not a single conscious memory on which to hang the feeling.

A couple of weeks passed, and Michele had another disturbing dream. In the morning she climbed out of bed and grabbed her black light. She was nearly shaking as she disrobed. She stepped into the closet so that no one would see her, and there she began to run the light over her body. Her stomach lurched when she saw the first orange mark. It was like a fluorescent fingerprint. She found others on her arms, legs, and torso.

Michele ran to the bathroom and tried to scrub the marks off, but they were still there. It took several days before the marks faded.

Michele began to examine her body after every one of her strange dreams. Each time she would find markings. Some were like fingerprints, some resembled three-fingered handprints, while others were like strange hieroglyphic writing. It reminded her of how doctors write on a person before surgery so that they know what they are doing.

Michele heard of a group of people who believed that they had survived UFO encounters, and she joined the discussions. There she heard many stories and came across others who would find the strange marks on their bodies after they were abducted or had dreamed that they were.

When her daughter came to her and told her about her own dreams of being abducted, Michele was shocked. Her dreams were extremely vivid and they were difficult to talk about because they were very personal and sometimes sexual in nature. Since then, Michele and her daughter have shared dreams on occasion. They can't explain how they have the same dreams on the same nights, but it does happen.

Michele is always careful to say that she was never abducted. She has no conscious memory of being taken, only those strange dreams. However, she has experienced other strange occurrences that she can't explain. She needed to have surgery on her hand and was shocked when the surgeon asked her how she had gotten a small metal pellet in her hand. Michele had no idea what he was talking about. She had never damaged that hand, and she had no knowledge of anything ever being broken off or implanted into her hand. Furthermore, she had no scar tissue to indicate the probable insertion site. The surgeon showed her the x-ray of a perfect little rod-shaped metal pellet. The pellet is in a nest of nerves, and she has chosen not to have it removed for fear it might reduce the dexterity in that hand.

Today the dreams still occasionally happen, but Michele has gained a calmness and a perspective on the events that keeps her composed. She does not believe that these beings are going to hurt her or her daughter. If they were, they'd have surely done so by now. However, it is a strange way to live. Michele helps others to put their own unnerving experiences into perspective, and she has become a font of knowledge and support for those who have nowhere to turn. And through it all, she has remained a charming and happy woman who has willingly told her strange story.

INCIDENT AT LYNDORA

September 10, 1996, was an average day in western Pennsylvania, but that night would begin one of the most widespread UFO sightings to ever take place in the region. It began at about 8:15 P.M., when dozens of people on Main Street in Butler saw a large, bright light high in the sky. It had just grown dark, and they watched what they would later describe as a "bright star or planet." Within minutes, the light began to change and drew much closer.

The observers were shocked to see a large, three-sided craft of some sort. The craft had five portholes or windows, with the largest one being in the center of the craft. Each of the windows glowed with golden light. The ship was outlined in blinking yellow, green, red, and blue lights. As the observers watched, a second, smaller craft became visible. It was designed exactly like the larger one with the five glowing windows. The smaller object also had the same colored lights outlining it.

Among those observing the objects were several people who had binoculars in their vehicles. They watched through the binoculars as the two craft separated and veered off in different directions. The larger craft moved very slowly toward the west while the smaller one headed east at a much faster pace. It was gone within moments, but the large craft lingered, barely moving for nearly half an hour.

The witnesses called the police, several UFO reporting centers, and family and friends. They had a great deal of time to observe the craft.

Suddenly, a solid beam of white light shot out of the triangular craft. The observers saw the beam on the ground, but no one dared to go near it. The entire time the object slowly moved westward. It was low in the sky and finally vanished behind a copse of trees. It was estimated that the craft was observed for nearly two hours.

Later it would be known that the craft came from the Lyndora area, where it had first been observed floating toward Butler. One of those who first sighted the craft in Lyndora was a state constable. He described the triangular craft as having bright white lights at the corners and small green and red lights toward the front. The craft floated over Butler and across the intersection of McCalmont Road and PA Route 8. The witnesses from Lyndora observed the craft for nearly forty minutes before they lost sight of it as it headed toward Butler.

Police officers responded to the multitude of telephone calls from concerned witnesses. There was a great deal of emergency radio chatter. Those who listened to the radio transmissions realized that the authorities were concerned and confused by the craft, too.

The police climbed to the top of a high-rise parking garage to watch the strange craft from a closer vantage point. They observed the craft through binoculars while reporting to a dispatcher what they were witnessing. The dispatcher reported to the officers on the scene that she was receiving multiple calls from civilian witnesses.

By now a large group of officers had amassed on the parking garage roof to watch the strange craft. At approximately 9:10 P.M., the object shot a beam of light that pinpointed the officers on the rooftop. Terrified, the officers scattered away from the light and reported to the dispatcher what had just happened.

Witnesses later told researchers that five minutes after the officers were dispersed by the light beam, the craft shot another light beam to the ground. By now, people were watching from the roof of the parking garage, the sidewalks, and a nearby mall. The craft finally disappeared after the second beam of light moved across the ground. Altogether, the craft was sighted from the ground for over two hours.

Downtown Butler was still in a frenzy at midnight. Police officers were all over the place, and the citizens who had seen the craft were still milling around talking and waiting for an official response.

To everyone's shock, the craft suddenly reappeared. Several people, including policemen, saw the craft hovering at the juncture of North Duffy Road and PA Route 356. They watched in awe as the craft moved westward again toward Moraine State Park. It was over the area of the park when it suddenly disappeared.

The reappearance caused a resurgence of interest in the object. It was extremely unusual for a UFO to appear once, but to have a craft appear for two hours, and then to have it return, was unprecedented.

Even more shocking, the craft made yet a third appearance that night. Around 3 A.M., patrons of a restaurant on PA Route 356 reported sighting the craft. Approximately twenty-five people tumbled out of the restaurant to watch the craft from the parking lot. The object moved in a northeasterly direction and was observed for half an hour.

The last known sighting of the craft came the following night, when a resident of Butler Township reported to police that a triangular craft with white lights at the corners was hovering over his neighbor's house.

Dan Hageman's group, the Butler Organization for Research of the Unexplained (BURO), began researching the sightings shortly after they began. BURO, Stan Gordon, and other UFO researchers in the area interviewed the many witnesses, the police officers, and others involved. This case remains one of the largest mass sightings in Pennsylvania history—and there has been no theory, no solution, and no explanation for what hovered over Butler County that night.

Ring Around the UFOs

Matt Covert and his buddy Keith sat down at a local bar in Butler on March 8, 1990, and ordered a beer. They saw another local, twenty-one-year-old Todd Thompson, and pushed their stools over slightly so Todd could sit down.

"What's shaking?" Matt asked.

Todd looked pretty rough. "Not much," he muttered as he slid into place and took a sip from the beer that was set in front of him.

The two friends chatted with Todd for a couple of minutes before he turned the conversation to what was really on his mind. "Man, Bryan, Ray, and I were out at the woods behind your mom's place this afternoon running our bikes when something freaking weird happened."

Todd took another gulp of beer. "Now I freely admit that we were drinking a lot, but up in the sky we suddenly saw these UFO things. I mean flying discs—and they were whirling around. I remember this strange pink haze and that's about it. I was plastered, but whatever they were, freaked us out. We took off. It was really creepy."

Matt and Keith exchanged glances. Todd was a bit of a rowdy, and had been known to embellish a story or two. But there was something about the look in Todd's eyes that told them that despite the beer, the guy was telling the truth—at least as he knew it.

"Look, guys," Todd said earnestly, "I know that no one will believe me. I don't want my name dragged into this if possible. I mean, I don't need the hassle, but you guys should check out the spot. Something strange is happening up there."

After Matt finished his drink he went out and got into his truck. It was about midnight and he should have gone home, but he knew the spot that Todd was talking about. His family owned an old farm that adjoined land owned by the Woodcock family. The Coverts didn't farm the land, and it had the highest hill in Butler County. Anyone with any kind of bike was allowed to use the trails and paths up there and ride around the fields. It was common knowledge that folks could use the place, and the dirt road up to the spot was well traveled.

Matt put the vehicle in drive and started off. Maybe he'd just take a look around and see what was going on up there tonight, he thought. He nosed the truck onto the road and eased his way up to the field. Matt stopped the truck where his lights could illuminate the field. He could barely believe what he saw. There were huge ovals burned into the field grass. The ovals were about eight or nine feet in diameter and there were several of them. He stared for a moment in disbelief. The hair stood up on his neck and he rammed the truck back into gear, turning around and spraying dirt behind him as he got out of there. For the first time in his life, Matt was afraid in the woods of his family farm.

The next morning Matt called his mother, Cheryl, at her job and talked her into leaving work to meet him at the spot. Cheryl explained to her boss that she had an emergency and left work at about 9 A.M. She stopped to pick up her camcorder on the way.

Cheryl was shocked by what she saw. There were nine circles imprinted on the ground. The vegetation within the circles was burned and depressions in the ground indicated that whatever had been there was very heavy. Cheryl's video from that morning was unaccountably filled with static. She and family members returned later that evening and filmed again. This time the video was much clearer, except for a "misting" around the outer edges of the frames. It had rained during the day and some of the family observed a "slimy" film in the circles. Jane Woodcock, the neighbor whose property bordered the area, also took video and hers was very clear, save for the fogging effect that once again appeared. This ruled out the effect as being a malfunction of a single camera.

In the next few days, others made their way to the site to snap photos and shoot video of the strange circles. The Pennsylvania Association for the Study of the Unexplained (PASU) was called in. The organization was run by the renowned Stan Gordon, a legend in paranormal research in western Pennsylvania.

The researchers dispatched to the case were Evelyn Schurman and John Gribble. The team had a local Radiological Defense Officer check the site for radioactivity, but there was none.

The Woodcocks and Coverts were questioned and every one of them agreed that they had never smelled anything unusual at the site—including the smell of burned grass. Several people had picked up hunks of burned grass but couldn't even smell smoke on it at that close range. Schurman burned some nearby grass, and unlike the grass in the circles, it did have a distinctive smell. The burned vegetation within the circles did not crumble; it seemed almost melted together. The burned vegetation outside of the circle did crumble.

According to the report, "At the beginning of the investigation we were all suspect of the rings being the creation of the mischief-making cyclists, but after close observation have set aside that assertion."

The team's observations brought to light several strange things. First, there were no divots or foot markings in the area. There were no other disturbances around the ovals. Also, the depth of the ovals was not uniform, indicating that more than one oval-shaped object was used or that it landed multiple times. Despite repeated questioning, none of the young men confessed to a hoax. There were no traces of accelerants found. Other experts called in to detect a hoax all indicated that they could not find any evidence to support that theory.

The belief is that there was most probably only one UFO that was rotating for some reason and set down multiple times. Why it did so is merely speculation, but the most obvious reason would be because of a malfunction. That might explain the burned areas as well. The team also noted in its report that the grass in the burned areas grew back three times as fast as the grass in the burned area outside the ovals. No explanation was offered as to why.

There was one new burned mark discovered on March 9, and it was more circular than oval. The conclusion was that possibly the bikers had made this circle, although they have consistently denied that.

The circles were not the only strange phenomena: on March 9, the *Butler Eagle* newspaper reported a large power outage in the area. There were also other reports of UFO sightings in the area at the approximate time of the primary sighting. Within months of the first report, eleven children and a bus driver all saw a UFO in the same general area, hovering near Hyland Golf Course. Cheryl Covert has reported seeing a UFO near the site on her property several times since then. People began watching for the UFO up in the woods and some of them have also reported sightings.

In the UFO report dated March 14, 1990, Schurman stated that when she and her team arrived at the site it was already dark and they were having a difficult time seeing to gather evidence. Then a glow started in the treeline. The light stayed stationary for a few minutes before it came into view. Two team members ran to their cars for their camcorders and captured two minutes of video, which showed an extremely bright light bouncing up and down. The light winked off and on a couple times, and then it shot off to the south at a high speed. The team could not determine what type of craft it was, but they had ruled out jets, helicopters, and other known aircraft. The total observation time for the light was about eleven minutes.

The team would later indicate that they felt "watched" during the whole time they were at the site. UFO investigators usually appear only after the events, and they rarely ever have any direct experiences themselves. It is an unusual and interesting case for many reasons, especially because the UFO returned multiple times and seemed to be monitoring those visiting the site.

FARM FIELD ENCOUNTER

Farming is hard work and often requires a great deal of dedication from the farmer. Spring planting can be a marathon of work, just as harvest season is. For one farmer in Butler County, May 7, 1998, will always be remembered not for the fact that he was up at 3:30 A.M. planting corn, but for what happened to him while he did so.

The farmer was driving his tractor up and down the fields, dragging a corn planting device that automatically dropped a kernel every few inches. He was exhausted but enjoying the cool night air. Suddenly, in the distance, he noticed lights moving through an adjacent wheatfield. The farmer paused for a second to watch. Was someone driving through his wheatfield? he wondered angrily. As the lights drew closer, there seemed to be more of them. The lights were square-shaped and there were five on each side. They flashed bright orange, pink, and blue. He realized with a fright that the craft containing the lights was nearly forty feet long and shaped so that it sloped down at the sides and had a dome on top. The lights ebbed and waned, but they never quite went out. A strange haze or vapor seemed to encompass the craft.

Suddenly the tractor began to sputter and cut out. The strange vehicle continued toward him through the wheatfield. A sensor on the corn planter began to malfunction, beeping incessantly. The farmer had to turn off the machine, but he barely took his eyes off the craft that was coming toward him.

The farmer watched in shock as the craft rose up and took off. It skimmed the treetops as it went aloft. The farmer knew that there were powerlines where the craft had lifted off, but he saw no sparking to indicate that it had hit the lines. The craft disappeared as suddenly as it had appeared.

The next day the farmer examined the area and found no sign of the craft. He later called in UFO investigators from the Butler Organization for Research of the Unexplained, and they also scoured the area for any signs of the event. However, all that was left was one very confused farmer.

The Kecksburg Incident

It was a cold, dreary afternoon on December 9, 1965, at the Kalp family farm outside of Kecksburg, a small village about forty miles away from Pittsburgh. The Kalp children were outside playing in a nearby field when they noticed an object streaking green fire across the sky. The object crashed in the woods on the far side of the field. The excited children ran to tell their mother about the plane crashing in the woods.

Francis Kalp saw the smoke rising from the woods and called for help. She then called John Murphy, news director of WHJB Radio at AM 620 in Greensburg. It was 6:30 P.M.

Across town, Bill Bulebush was working on his car. He heard a hissing sound and looked up to see an acorn-shaped object spouting yellow-red fire with a green vapor trail about two hundred feet in the air. Bulebush wasn't sure what the object was, but it was about twice as large as a Volkswagen Beetle and seemed to be under intelligent control. It was gliding slowly before it made a U-turn and headed toward the woods, where it then went down.

The Pennsylvania State Police headed for the scene of the crash. John Murphy also hurried to the scene, and he arrived before the police and fire department got there. He went down to the crash site and took photographs. Amazed by the bronze-colored, acorn-shaped craft, he finished out one roll of film and began another. John heard people moving toward the scene and hurried up the hill to meet the authorities, including state troopers, Fire Marshal Carl Metz, and military officers. John would later say that his film was confiscated from the camera, but no one knew that he had a full roll in his pocket. He called his wife on the CB radio from the crash site that night and indicated to her that he had the film.

Murphy attempted to get information from the fire marshal, who ordered the woods cordoned off. When Metz came back from viewing the site, Murphy asked him what was down there. Metz replied, "I'm not sure. You'd better get your information from the Army."

James Romansky was a young fireman among the volunteer firefighters called out to help locate the crash site in the woods. He would later describe what he saw. He claimed that when he got to the crash site, the tops of the trees were broken and rocks and dirt were furrowed in a long, gouged-out area where the craft had slid. The craft had come to rest against a little hillock. Romansky said that the craft was acorn-shaped and had hieroglyphic-like writing around its bottom ring. The craft was on its side and he could not see a window, door, or opening in the craft. Years later, Romansky would describe the craft for a documentary done by renowned researcher Stan Gordon: "It had writing on it, not like your average writing, but more like ancient Egyptian hieroglyphics. It had sort of a bumper on it, like a ribbon about six to ten inches wide, and it stood out. It was elliptical the whole way around, and the writing was on this bumper. It's nothing like I've ever seen, and I'm an avid reader. I read a lot of books on Egypt, the Incas, Peruvians, and Russians and I've never to this day come across anything that looked like that."

Romansky would later say that within fifteen minutes of his arrival, government and military men appeared and ordered the volunteer firemen away from the scene. He went back up the hill and discovered that the military had taken over the scene. Armed soldiers established a perimeter around the top of the hill.

Murphy returned to his office and telephoned the state police barracks to obtain information. He was informed that the 662nd Radar Squadron from the Oakdale Army Support Facility was at the site and that they were going to release a statement regarding the crash in Kecksburg. When Murphy arrived at the police barracks, he saw both Air Force and Army personnel in the barracks. The official statement was, "The Pennsylvania State Police have made a thorough investigation of the woods. We are convinced there is nothing whatsoever in the woods."

John Murphy accompanied the police and military personnel back to the woods, where he saw uniformed men with scientific equipment going down to the crash site. He found that the woods had been declared off limits.

Young newspaper reporter Bob Gatty arrived at the crash site only to find that it was quarantined by uniformed Army personnel. He was challenged and forced back when he tried to get further details.

Lillian Hays and her husband lived in a farmhouse not far from the crash site, and their home became a command post for military and government officials. Throughout the evening, the officials repeatedly made phone calls, and Lillian worried that she would have a terrible phone bill. When the bill later arrived, no calls from that night were on it.

Lillian's son, John, was ten years old, and he and his siblings were kept upstairs that night. However, they had a good vantage point to watch as people came and went from the house and into the woods. He maintained that he saw Air Force personnel, Army officers, and people with NASA patches on their white coveralls. He also testified that he saw a flatbed truck go into the woods through the nearby field. The truck was empty going in, but when it came out it had a large object strapped to it and covered with a tarp. The next day, John and his brother went into the area to see what they could find. A man with what John called a "metal detector" yelled at them and told them to go back home because there could be radiation down there.

Time after time, curious local folks were approached by military men with guns who turned them away. Local resident Bill Weaver drove to the site and saw four men in "moon suits," or white coveralls, carrying a 4 x 6 box down to the crash site. When the teenager went for the spotlight in his car to see better, a soldier turned him back.

Mable Mazza was working at the WHJB radio station that night and was shocked by the volume of phone calls that she received. First military and government officials called for directions, and then the calls from other media outlets began. All of them were converging on Kecksburg (also called Acme in some reports, after a nearby village). At one point, ABC News in New York announced that a UFO had crashed in Kecksburg, Pennsylvania. Shortly thereafter, the staff at the radio station, which was an ABC affiliate, received a phone call from the network telling them to no longer mention the crash; they also instructed the staff to pass the order on to John Murphy.

Robert Blystone Jr. was sixteen years old at the time and went to the crash site. He later said that there were "military everywhere." He also stated that inquisitive onlookers were warned to turn back by the perimeter guards.

Jerry Betters was a young jazz musician from Pittsburgh. He heard the account of the UFO on the radio and convinced a couple friends to drive to Kecksburg and check it out. He saw armed military men all over, and there was a flatbed truck coming out of the woods with a large, covered object on it. Suddenly a military officer saw the young men and shouted to a soldier, "Get these people out of here!" Betters said of the soliders, "They were pretty nasty with us. They turned the guns on us." Betters and his friends left at that point.

John Murphy's wife, Bonnie, would later tell investigators about John's film, saying, "I know that John had pictures of the object—he told me he did." She would state that despite the fact that "this was like the story of his lifetime," John suddenly stopped talking about it three weeks later.

In the days after the crash John Murphy put together a radio special called *Object in the Woods*. In the last couple days before the documentary was to air, John Murphy received several calls from people he had interviewed for the show. They all indicated that they wanted their interviews cut from the show. They stated that they were afraid of the state police or that they "didn't want to get in trouble with the Army." By the time the special aired, much of the content was altered.

A few days after the episode aired, some men visited Murphy at work. They appeared to be professional men and when they left, Murphy was very upset. He told the staff at the station that the men took his taped interviews. After that, he stopped talking about the events of that night. When people brought it up, he would quickly change the subject.

Bonnie Murphy noticed that all of John's notes were suddenly gone from the house, as well. She never saw the photographs that he had taken. John was struck and killed by a hit-and-run driver in 1969 in Ventura, California. Before his death, he gave a copy of the original, unedited documentary to researcher Stan Gordon, but Stan discovered that it went missing after John's death.

There were dozens upon dozens of people who saw what happened or part of what happened that night. Firefighters, businesspeople, entertainers, police officers, and reporters all testify to the same series of events. Something large fell in the woods outside of Kecksburg and the military was extremely anxious to go in and secure the area so that they could remove it. A large flatbed truck went into the woods empty and returned with a large object secured on it under heavy tarps. A farmhouse and the fire station were used as staging areas for the military and NASA workers who retrieved the object. Fire Marshal Carl Metz would be asked about that night many times and he would always state that he was sworn to secrecy by an Army officer.

There are several theories about what actually fell in the woods that night. The official explanation was that a meteorite had plummeted to the ground. There are many flaws with this theory. Louis Winker of the Penn State Department of Astronomy stated in an interview with Stan Gordon that there was a Geminid meteor shower at that time, but it was highly unlikely that anything would have survived the trip through Earth's atmosphere to crash in Kecksburg. He further argued that the size of the object described should have caused a crater if it had plunged to the earth. Furthermore, the military response to the "meteor" was unprecedented.

Officially, the only military presence there that night were three men from Project Blue Book, an Air Force program concerning UFOs. A military report from Project Blue Book does exist, but its findings fly in the face of witness reports. Numerous local citizens saw a significant military presence at the scene that night.

Another theory is that the event was the reentry of Cosmos 96, a Soviet satellite. It is known that Cosmos 96 did reenter the atmosphere that same afternoon. It was tracked across Canada and the eastern United States. Years later, UFO researcher and former military officer Clifford Stone had an opportunity to speak with former Soviet officials about the Kecksburg crash. He was told that the Soviet Union had been tracking the satellite and that officials there believe that something from outer space struck the satellite and knocked it out of orbit. They believe that the object that went down in Kecksburg was the same object that had struck the satellite. They insisted that they knew where the satellite went down, and it was not in Kecksburg.

Some speculate that the object was a Nike missile shot straight up in the air, but none of the eyewitness accounts substantiate that theory. There is no record of such a missile launched on that night. Others claim that it was a spy plane, but again, there is no evidence that such a plane ever existed. The eyewitness accounts do not describe a plane at all.

Even those who saw the craft do not agree on what crashed in Kecksburg that night. What is clear is that something large did crash or emergency land in the woods outside of Kecksburg. Whatever it was, it brought out the military from several different branches in unprecedented numbers. The object was taken away and a cover-up began.

The best source for eyewitness accounts of the Kecksburg story is the DVD *Kecksburg: The Untold Story*. It was made by Stan Gordon, who is world renowned for his research on the crash often dubbed "Pennsylvania's Roswell."

Close Encounters of the Third Kind

C lose Encounters of the Third Kind are by far the most unnerving. These encounters involve sightings of the occupants of UFOs. I have also placed cases of abduction and experimentation in this category. These are often terrifying and traumatic stories. However, it must be noted that some abductions do not engender fear at all. It is puzzling what occurs when these alien beings and humans interact.

The Mysterious Tale of Josephine Francis

In November 1967, while most folks were preparing for the holiday season, forty-one-year-old Indiana County resident Josephine Francis was not focused on Thanksgiving. Francis was struggling through a life-shattering series of events—she had been abducted by strange creatures.

Josephine was pregnant that November, and she and her husband were raising their daughter and preparing for the birth of their second child. On the night when the events began, Josephine was going through her normal routine. She put her daughter to bed and settled down to relax for a few minutes before going to bed herself. She was exhausted, but that was because of the pregnancy and the fact that she spent her days chasing after a very active child.

Around 10 P.M., Josephine got ready for bed and gratefully lay down. Her husband had already gone to bed and she curled up beside him expecting nothing more than to wake up to a normal day the following morning.

Suddenly Josephine became aware of the world around her. She was in the woods outside of her home alongside a strange man. Josephine looked around and realized that she was dressed only in her nightgown and her feet were bare, yet she felt strangely calm. She felt almost removed from the situation. It was cold out but she didn't feel that either. Josephine would later tell investigators, "We were walking toward an object sitting on the ground and it was very dark except for the dull light that came from the thing."

Josephine calmly moved forward with the man and observed him. He was short, not much more than five feet tall, and he had a dark complexion. The man's clothes were dark shadows over his body that she could not initially make out due to the lighting conditions. The man spoke to her and urged her to get to the craft.

Josephine raised her eyes and dispassionately studied the craft she was walking toward. The ship was squatting about fifteen feet off the ground on three tubular legs supported by wide, round, bowl-like feet. The craft itself was round and gleamed silver in the faint light that it was emitting from its underside. There were no clues as to the origins of the craft. No writing, markings, or symbols could be seen on the seamless, smooth curves of the craft. There seemed to be no windows or doors through which a person could look into or enter the craft.

As they reached the ship, the man instructed Josephine to follow him. He stepped beneath the craft and she followed. At that time she saw the clothes that the man wore—a dark shirt, pants, and sweater. He wore a dark cap on his head.

Josephine saw that there was a metal ladder coming from the bottom of the craft that led up into an opening. The man indicated that she should grasp the first rung of the ladder. It was hard for Josephine to pull her pregnant body up the ladder, and the man helped her up.

Inside the craft a softly diffused light illuminated the area, but Josephine saw no lighting source. She looked around but saw very little. The man spoke to her and she followed him obediently into a room.

That room was softly illuminated as well, but again there was no source for the lighting. The only piece of furniture she saw was a desk. Josephine was drawn to the desk and saw a "logbook" lying on the desk. She would later say that she could not remember seeing English words but she somehow understood what was written in the logbook.

An alien being suddenly appeared in the room. The figure was short and stocky like the man who had led Josephine to the craft. There were four or five other beings who followed the leader into the room. They were dressed alike in dark shirts with large buttons and black pants without belts. The only difference was that the leader had a different cap. They had rounded faces with large, black, slanted eyes. Josephine saw no whites in the eyes but she could see when the eyes shifted. The creatures had slits where their noses should have been. They had no lips, leaving the impression that their mouths were just holes. They naturally held their mouths shut, creating slits. They had dark brown, rough skin that Josephine described as "alligator-like." The creatures had no hair.

Josephine gasped as the leader lunged at her and shoved her away from the logbook. The being seemed very angry as it approached her. She again didn't remember hearing English, but she did understand what the leader was saying. He told her to forget what she saw in the book, and she was surprised that she instantly could not recall what she had just read.

Josephine realized that she was hearing the beings in her head telepathically; this was how they communicated. She heard them tell her to follow them. Josephine should have been terrified, but she felt numb and simply did as she was told.

In the next room there was a wide metallic table and Josephine understood that she needed to climb atop it. She suddenly found herself on the table, nude, but could remember neither undressing nor climbing onto the table.

She tried to move her hands to cover her naked body but found that the beings had secured her hands with large cloth bonds. She could feel the coldness of the table and she struggled to move but was pinned down somehow. Josephine was cold, humiliated, and terrified.

The beings gathered around her, seeming to observe her. The man who had brought her to the craft stood quietly inside the room watching and waiting as the creatures began to touch her. Six months pregnant, Josephine began to worry about her baby. Were they interested in the child?

Frightened now, Josephine watched as a thin rod was slipped under one of her fingernails. Attached to the cylinder was a larger "straw" that collected blood. Then the creatures took a sharp object and scraped her abdomen in several places. They laid the scrapings on a plate. Josephine was aware of the pain and the pressure, but it felt faint and distant. What were they doing—and why?

The creatures then forced her leg into a large, spring-like device. The device had a rod on one end with a pointed object that pricked her stomach. The device began to vibrate around her leg. She heard the leader speaking in her head. He told her that she needed to lay still. He explained that they wanted the child. The pointed object was a diamond tip that they were going to insert into her uterus and into the brain of the child. He told her that the child was a girl and that he wanted Josephine's consent to begin the procedure. The child would stay with her for a while before they took it, he informed her. Then he told her that they had tried this procedure before but that the results were not always good. Some of the children had died because they had inserted the diamond tip at the wrong time or because the mother did not stay still. Now they needed her consent to take the child.

Josephine argued and struggled against her bonds, wiggling and shouting as she fought for her child's life. The leader grew angrier and angrier, and it became a battle of wills. The furious leader then stormed out of the room, followed by the other creatures.

Josephine was left exhausted and alone with the human who had brought her to the craft. He came forward and stood near her. He tried to calm her and told her that if she fought they couldn't take the baby.

The leader came back in the room, his aggravation evident. Again he tried to talk her into giving him the child. She continued to argue— wriggling, squirming, and yelling.

After an indeterminate amount of time, the leader stormed off again. The others hurried after him, and they stood in a far corner of the room discussing the situation. They agreed that it was almost dawn and they needed to get Josephine home.

The next thing Josephine remembered was waking up in her own bed, exhausted. When she awoke, there were small cuts on her feet and legs. Her muscles hurt, and she struggled to get through the day.

Josephine tried to tell her husband what had happened to her but he did not want to hear it. He told her that it was just a bad dream.

She showed him the scratches across her belly and legs and he got very upset. He refused to discuss the matter at all and declared it complete foolishness.

Josephine remained alone with her experience. Her husband's rejection of the events made her even more upset. She did give birth to a little girl and she tried to concentrate on her children. She pushed her strange experience into the back of her mind until 1972.

That year, Josephine walked into a shoe store in Indiana on a hazy summer afternoon and found herself staring in shock at the short, stocky shoe salesman. It was the man who had led her to the craft that night five years earlier. The man's eyes met hers and he was visibly startled. She was sure that he recognized her. Shocked and frightened, she turned and ran out of the store.

For the entire afternoon she argued with herself about what had just happened. Finally she decided to return to the store and confront the man. She needed answers and this man could give them to her. She waited outside for the man to leave the building, but eventually the owner locked up for the day, and the man had not come out.

Josephine approached the manager and he shrugged. "You must be talking about Joe Smith. He left early today. Come back tomorrow and you should be able to talk to him."

The next day Josephine returned to the store, but the man from the craft did not show up. For days she returned but Joe Smith never came back to work, nor did he call in. He simply vanished.

Josephine questioned the store owner and went to the rooming house where Joseph Smith lived. However, he never returned to his apartment, either. Researchers would later contact every Joseph Smith in the area, but none of them came even close to Josephine's description of the short, pudgy man.

In 1983, Josephine would begin having further encounters. In the spring of that year, Josephine's now teenage daughter, Jenny, awoke to find four strange figures in her bedroom one night. Jenny was the child that Josephine had been carrying when she was abducted.

Jenny shared the room with a younger sister, and she had not heard about her mother's strange experience because Josephine had still not spoken about it. It was her secret, and she had never wanted to frighten her children with the terrifying experience.

On the night of her encounter, Jenny saw the figures with the big black eyes, the holes for mouths and the slits where their noses should have been, and she let out a terrified scream. She tried to roll over and run but she was somehow pinned or frozen in place. She couldn't move at all. She was sure that her parents would hear her screams and come to help her but no one came. The beings produced two long, pointed instruments and they inserted them into her ears despite her best efforts to resist.

Jenny could feel the pain and she screamed louder. The pain was excruciating and she began to cry. Still her parents did not respond. The beings imparted to her mentally that they were going to take her with them. Jenny argued and refused. At that point the beings seemed to get upset and they left. The moment they were gone, Jenny was no longer pinned and she jumped up and ran down the stairs to her mother. Behind Jenny came her younger sister, who was also crying.

Josephine and her oldest daughter were still up and they were shocked by the two terrified girls. In broken sobs Jenny told her story. Her little sister confirmed the story. She had seen the entire thing from her bed but she had been paralyzed, too.

Josephine touched her daughter's ears and there was blood on them. They would later find blood on her pillow, too. Josephine felt her heart freeze. No one knew her story, but still she chose to take a skeptical view. The girls had just had a nightmare or something and she tried to convince them of that. Neither of the girls would accept that explanation. They *had* seen the creatures.

Jenny grabbed a pen and paper and sketched what she had seen. Josephine took the paper from her daughter and found her legs giving out. Staring at her from the page was a crude sketch of the very figures she had seen so long ago. Jenny had also drawn the devices that they had inserted into her ears. On the end of the one rod was a diamond-tipped device exactly like the one that Josephine had seen years earlier. It was the device that the leader had tried to insert into her unborn child's brain!

Jenny's description of the dark, alligator-skinned beings caused Josephine to tremble. What had they done to her daughter? Why had they returned now? Would they come back? Would they take Jenny?

Josephine's husband did not believe the story. He blamed it on Josephine, for telling the girls her nightmare from long ago. Josephine argued that she had never told anyone. She showed her husband the bloody pillowcase. He countered that Jenny had simply scratched her ears.

Josephine's worst fears came true. The creatures returned several times to her home. The first time, Jenny and her little sister saw the beings on the roof outside the bedroom window. They were smiling and laughing. They tried to coax Jenny outside to go with them but she refused. They paid no attention to the smaller girl.

The next visit Jenny experienced was even stranger. On that night she awoke to find her boyfriend standing over her. He leaned down and kissed her. He asked her to go with him and indicated the open window. Jenny couldn't understand that, because she and her sister had been locking the window and pulling the curtains every night since the first visit. Jenny refused to go with her boyfriend, and he suddenly changed into one of the creatures. It again tried to convince her to accompany it, but she refused.

On another night she awoke to see six of the beings in the room. They once again produced the rods and tried to force them into her ears. She again struggled but was paralyzed. This time she remembered a strong "antiseptic" smell when the rods got close to her head.

The visits continued from April through August of that year. Weeks could go by without a visit, and then the creatures would show up multiple times in one week. Jenny would later tell investigators that there were clearly two leaders. There was a gentle one who comforted her and another one that was highly agitated and upset when she refused to leave with them. She would see them enter her room through the closed and locked window, and they always seemed bent upon taking her with them.

On one occasion, she awoke to find only the comforting being in the room. He never forced her to do anything and never caused her pain. He explained to her that it was important that she go with them. Jenny still refused and the being simply left.

During that time, Josephine sought out help for her family. Despite her husband's condemnation, she found Dr. Paul Johnson and told him the story. Dr. Johnson researched the case, but there was little he could do for the family, and he deemed it one of the strangest alleged abduction cases that he and his team ever worked on.

The Little Brown Men

It was a cool October night in 1944, and the Radnor family were all asleep in their home, a farmhouse in the country outside of Rochester, Beaver County. A loud crash and sudden flash of light disturbed the chill night air. The family tumbled out of bed. They had all heard the sound and seen the bright flash of light outside their remote home.

Mrs. Radnor huddled the children together as Mr. Radnor pulled on his pants and boots. Something was going on outside and he planned to find out exactly what. He hurried downstairs and pulled the door open. Mr. Radnor froze in surprise. Standing on the other side of the door was a small figure about four and a half feet tall. The figure was humanoid and robed, but unlike any human that he had ever seen. About fifteen feet away to the left were five more figures of similar size and appearance; however, these figures were wearing "luminous, brown, metallic suits," according to Mr. Radnor. These beings also glowed softly.

Mr. Radnor would later describe the figures, saying, "Their heads were quite large. Their arms were long with long, thin fingers." He recalled that they had slits for mouths, and they seemed to exude a soft light from around their bodies.

The robed figure seemed to be the leader and he stepped forward. Mr. Radnor backed away as the figure approached. Two of the five other beings stepped forward and followed the robed figure into the house, after which they led Mr. Radnor out into the night.

Mr. Radnor found himself walking through the darkness behind the three beings. They took him to a large craft of some sort that was sitting near the farmhouse. Mr. Radnor felt dazed, almost as if the incident was happening to someone else.

He would not remember anything else until morning, when he awoke in his bed badly shaken. He glanced around the room but everything seemed fine. "It had to be a dream," he told himself as he sat up in bed. He stumbled to the bathroom, dressed, and listened as his wife padded down the hall to make breakfast.

Mr. Radnor tried to shake off the terrible dream. He couldn't even explain why it was terrible, other than that it seemed so real. It simply had been a bad dream.

Suddenly Mrs. Radnor let out a strangled cry. "David, what on earth happened out there?"

Mr. Radnor ran down the stairs in the half light of early morning and found his wife staring out a window. He looked out, feeling certain that he wouldn't like what he was about to see. About twenty-five feet from the house was a large circle burned in the grass. The burned area was a perfect circle over twenty-five feet in diameter. It hadn't been a dream after all.

The time frame makes this story very compelling. Many of the features we now note as common to UFO encounters are present in this story, but it happened at a time when UFOs were not widely spoken about. The family would have had little chance to read and falsely incorporate any popular themes in their story.

GREENSBURG ENCOUNTER

Mandy Epstein looked at the clock and sighed. It had been a long night for the young woman. She had agreed to babysit her next-door neighbor's little boy for the evening while the neighbor worked. It was February of 1981, and despite the heat pouring in through the vents, the cold wind outside chilled Mandy.

She flipped the channel again on the television and glanced once more at the clock. Her husband would be leaving for work at 1:45 A.M. It was that time now, and so Mandy got up and walked out to the screened-in porch to look for her husband. Mandy didn't see the car or her husband, but what she did see made her freeze. She looked up at a large, triangular craft moving silently over the housetops about fifty feet above roof level. The object had a large light at each point of the triangle. She could see what appeared to be stacks on top of the craft. There were windows across the craft, and what appeared to be metal partitions or levels inside the craft. The bottom of the ship glowed a soft white. As Mandy watched, the glowing white light seemed to separate and drop away from the craft. It lowered until it reached the street. She later compared the intensity of the white light to a weak flashlight beam.

Mandy stared in shock at the craft. In the front windows she could see two human-like beings. She was certain that they weren't people, though. She described them as having "very large heads, oriental-like eyes, gill-like ears, and two holes instead of a nose." She could see them clearly in the light the object emitted.

Mandy felt constrained not to move. She watched as the craft got closer. She could see that one being was sitting at a lighted panel. She could see only the hands and the head of the creature well. The seated being was working slide bars. White light glowed upward and a screen near it also glowed white, and Mandy could also see triangular buttons that appeared black or gray.

The second being was standing near the first one, and Mandy could see the upper torso of this second being. This creature was not wearing any clothing on its top half. It had a long thin neck, broad shoulders, smooth white skin, and normal-looking arms. The figure seemed to be moving its arms over an area that was not lit up. The creature studied her with white eyes that had no pupils.

Mandy was finally able to turn away after a while, although it took great will to do so. She hurried inside and locked the door. She was shaken and upset as she sat down and tried to think of what she should be doing. She felt somehow lethargic and unable to think clearly.

Suddenly the television let out a loud buzzing sound and flipped off. At the same moment the lamp blinked out, too. Mandy ran toward the kitchen, which was still lit. She grabbed the phone and dialed her parents' number. She poured out an incoherent story through her sobs and begged her folks to get her and the boy. When she hung up, she realized that she'd need to get the child. She ran up and got the boy out of bed.

Mandy's father pulled up at 2:50 A.M. and tried to calm his daughter. He loaded her and the child into the car. He could clearly see that his daughter was very upset, but he saw nothing out of the ordinary.

When the homeowner returned, she found the television on and the house vacated. The lamp light had burned out.

Mandy's father was convinced that something untoward had happened to his daughter and he telephoned the Pennsylvania State Police. They listened to the story, and then directed the family to the Pennsylvania Center for UFO Research.

The field researcher who interviewed the young woman found her to be "honest and reliable with no apparent motive for hoaxing." The interviewer's notes indicated that he was struck by Mandy's story. She seemed to be able to remember some things in great detail while other things were a complete blank to her. She also seemed to be unable to judge time during the event.

Despite the long duration of Mandy's sighting, no one else seemed to have seen the craft and creatures. Mandy remained steadfast in her story despite being ridiculed and laughed at. Certainly the young woman had some sort of experience, but the rest can be only speculation. How could she remember details like the pupil-less eyes and the control boards if she had not been closer to them? Was she in the craft but unable to remember? What about Mandy's confusion and the missing time? Those are common questions for those who encounter UFO's.

Why I Missed My Anniversary

Raymond Watson was feeling pleased with himself that cold winter afternoon in January of 1968. It was January 17, his wedding anniversary. Ray had just picked up his paycheck and was planning to cash it and go home to pick up his wife for a lovely anniversary evening. Jenny, his wife, had hired a babysitter for the occasion.

Ray made the turn onto Warren Road outside Indiana. Familiar scenery flashed by, but then something changed. In a field there was a large vehicle, squat and still—and hovering fifty feet off the ground. Ray jammed his foot down on the brake and the car came to a lurching stop. He rolled down the window and stared. Ray had never seen anything like what he was now seeing. The floating object was a large saucer-shaped craft between thirty and forty feet in diameter. There was a large windshield wrapped around part of the vehicle. Through the windshield, Ray could see two seated figures. Ray claimed that the figures acted excited to see him.

It was 3 P.M. when Ray first sighted the craft. It was 7 P.M. when Ray finally got home. He was confused and he could not account for those four hours. He was visibly shaken and unsettled. His wife was upset that he had forgotten the anniversary, but after she saw his face she realized that something very strange had happened. She listened in horror to Ray's story of seeing the UFO and the two humanoid figures inside of it.

At that time all Ray could remember was seeing the craft and slowing down; then it suddenly became dark. He felt himself coasting along in a cold, dark car, looking out at the craft and the two males figures inside it. They were slowly pulling four levers that were closely set together. As they pulled the levers, the craft gradually faded from view.

The Watsons were very upset by what Ray had seen, and they soon after contacted the Pennsylvania Center for UFO Research. The center began work on the case and, eventually, Ray agreed to be hypnotized in an attempt to fill in the missing time. What he remembered under hypnosis was compelling.

According to Ray, he pulled the car off the road and watched the craft from his open window. He was amazed by what he saw. His next memory was of walking through the woods and snow with one of the men from the craft. He described the figures as average-looking men. The man with Ray wore a very tight-fitting suit that reminded Ray of a scuba diver's wet suit. The strange figure reached out and touched Ray's hand. Ray said that the man's skin had a very soft feel, and once the man had his hand Ray felt that his independent will just melted away. The figure never moved his mouth, but rather spoke in Ray's head. "Come with me," he told Ray.

Ray responded, "No. I don't want to go." But he found himself drawn along, moving without his own determination. He was suddenly frightened by this figure. How was it making him move?

Ray remembered walking through the snow, but he felt no cold. He didn't feel the scrape of the brush as they moved into the field, either. He only felt that too-soft hand, and that he had to do what he was told. He tried to move his hands and arms and could do so, but it was difficult and felt as if he was moving against his own will. A set of steps were telescoping away from the ship. They were angled and flat and each step was braced against the one below it. Ray got the idea that when the steps folded up they would not be seen from outside.

Ray then entered the ship. The man seemed to hear his thoughts and spoke into his mind. Ray was told to step into a cylindrical tube. He did so and found himself in an elevator with the man. The elevator shot upward to the compartment where the two figures had been. It was a control room of some sort. There were panels with lights but no toggle switches, buttons, or other control mechanisms that he could see, except for a panel with four levers on it. Ray got the impression that the craft was malfunctioning and he believed that they were detaining him until they were done repairing it.

Near the elevator was a large box about three feet long and two and a half feet wide. It was pulled out and two men were working in it. There were modules plugged in and buttons and switches inside the box. One of the men working in the box was over six feet tall; the other was much shorter, approximately five and a half feet tall. They wore suits similar to that of the man who had brought Ray aboard, but they were gray or brown.

Ray walked over to the panels and stood there as directed. He glanced around, trying to take everything in. He saw a panel in the wall that looked like a computer of some sort. It was about two feet long and seemed to be a separate unit. There were English letters on the screen, spelling "SULCO." He could see out the windshield, and he could hear the men talking in his head.

The men were not paying any attention to Ray as they worked. They'd make repairs to the box, and then the man at the levers would slowly push the four of them at the same time. The ship would glow a hazy white and Ray could no longer see outside. When the man at the controls eased the levers back, the ship stopped glowing and Ray could see out again.

Ray believed that he had to stop the figures. He had to do something. A small, three-by-five-inch module was lying on a counter near him. Ray struggled to make his hand and arm move to grab it. He took the module in his hand and then eased it into his pocket. He needed something that would prove what he was seeing. As the module settled into his pocket, the figures turned and the one who seemed to be his keeper came toward him. He took the module back and told Ray to behave and not to cause trouble, or he'd be put in a place where he couldn't interfere.

Soon after, the man watching Ray told him to get back onto the elevator and they went down to another area. There, he heard a voice tell him to sit down but he saw no one. He had the impression that someone was in the room, but that person was not visible to him.

Ray saw only one chair in the room, and it reminded him of a barber's chair. He sat down and tried to think. He felt that he had to disable the ship. The chair seemed to be suctioned to the floor in some way. He wondered if he could break the suction and slow down the craft. If he could slow it down, maybe someone else would see it and get help.

Suddenly the voice spoke in his head again. It told him that he was causing too much trouble and he had to stop. The chair began to spin and Ray felt himself getting motion sick. The chair spun faster and faster.

Ray's next memory was of the cold. He was suddenly outside and terribly cold. He feared he was going to die of exposure and he tried to move his feet. He was about thirty feet from the craft. He made his way to his car and got in. The window was still down and the car seemed to be drifting along even though it was off. He struggled to get the car started. Ray drove home and it was there that Jenny informed him that he was four hours late and their night was ruined.

Ray's experience was terrifying and it certainly changed his life. He would never know who or what he encountered on the road that night when he missed his anniversary for a most incredible reason.

EXTRATERRESTIALS GO SHOPPING

Barbara considered herself an average sixty-five-year-old woman. She had seen a lot of life. In fact, Barbara had been forced to adapt to many changes, one of the hardest being when she found herself wheelchair-bound. But Barbara was not the sort to give up, and so she wouldn't allow those challenges to change the way she lived her life.

In June of 2008, she and her husband decided to go shopping at the Century III Mall near West Mifflin. Barbara's husband wasn't big on shopping, so he opted to sit on a bench and wait while she went into a department store.

Barbara made her way to the men's department and was a bit amused to see a mother hustle past her. The woman was hurrying and huddling her children together. The little boy was dragging his feet. "I want to see!" he cried as his mother dragged him along. "No, we need to leave now!" his mother admonished him. Barbara wondered what the dispute had been about.

She made the turn around some clothing racks and stopped dead. Standing before her was a male figure wearing blue pants and a plaid shirt. The being was not human, though. It was bald and wrinkled. The figure had bumps all over his gray skin, and his eyes were very dark and almond-shaped.

Barbara did a double-take and in that brief second the figure moved much closer to her. He faced her now and gave her a gentle smile. Barbara struggled not to stare, thinking that maybe this was a man with some terrible condition. She quickly shifted her eyes away, then right back again. In that brief span, the figure disappeared. Barbara hurried to a cashier. She was agitated and asked if a security guard could be called. She explained that she was looking for a man who had been in the men's department. The security guard allowed her to view the tape with him but there was no one to be seen in the area after she entered it.

Barbara's husband rejoined her and insisted that they had to go. By now Barbara was rattled and frightened. Exactly what had she seen?

Barbara and her husband had been planning to view a movie at the theater in the mall, and so they continued on with their plans. When she tried to explain what had happened to her, he insisted that they had to hurry not to miss the movie. He would listen to her story later. Barbara spent the rest of her time in the mall scanning faces for the little, gray, wrinkle-skinned being, but she never saw him again.

By the time the couple got home that night, Barbara had decided not to mention what she had seen earlier in the day. It was just too unnerving. The entire incident eventually seemed to slip from her mind.

Her experience remained unthought-of until one day in early October when Barbara opened the *Pittsburgh Tribune Review* newspaper and froze. Her eyes had been scanning down the columns when she saw an article about a UFO sighting.

Suddenly Barbara's hands began to shake. Deep in her mind something was stirring. She couldn't have explained how she knew, but she was certain that the being had repressed her memories of seeing him.

Barbara told her family about what she had seen, and then she contacted the western Pennsylvania branch of the Mutual UFO Network. Regional MUFON director John Ventre interviewed her. He looked into the case and found that on the same evening that Barbara had her strange encounter, someone else had reported seeing a UFO in the area of the mall.

It sounds like an incredible tale, but Ventre would later write about the case, "Normally, I would write this report off as a hoax, but she never changed her story and was completely convinced that she saw an extraterrestrial being."

THE STRANGE EXPERIENCE AT BOSWELL

Boswell is a small town in the Appalachian Mountains of Somerset County. The town was created as a mining community, and at its apex the local coal mine employed approximately nine hundred men. In the late 1930s, the mine failed and the town lost its major employment source. Since then, the town has shrunk to its present-day population of approximately 1,480 people. During that time, many interesting things occurred in tiny Boswell, but there was not a single event that could be considered stranger than what happened to a couple named George and Edna on the night of July 16, 1996.

On that night, George and Edna were at their home enjoying the evening. They had lived in the area for some time, and they liked the rural community and their neighbors.

In cities, light pollution often makes it difficult to see and enjoy the nighttime sky, but in Somerset County there is not a lot of light pollution. Consequently, many folks enjoy sitting outside on warm nights and gazing up at the beautiful, twinkling stars on their bed of black velvet.

It was a perfect summer night and it seemed that most of the neighborhood was out enjoying the cool air. Suddenly, George and Edna saw five pulsing diamonds of light in the sky. The objects moved with tremendous speed. The objects abruptly dropped down to about 180 feet above the ground and they began to pulse red, blue, and green. Not only did George and Edna see the lights, but several neighbors did, too. They all stopped to stare in amazement at the lights which were so close that they could see every detail of the glossy bodies of the objects.

George had fought in World War II and was known to be an unflappable fellow, but he felt a wave of fear wash over him. In his whole life he had never seen anything like those five lighted craft. He reached behind himself to the stand where he kept binoculars and slowly pulled them up to his eyes. He deftly adjusted the view and saw the five lighted craft come sharply into focus. He felt compelled to watch the pulsing lights. The fear swallowed him and he couldn't move. What on earth were the craft?

The five objects shot upward at a great rate of speed and George craned his neck to find the craft again. From out of the darkness three jets zoomed into view. The five craft seemed to respond to the arrival of the planes by quickly flying away.

George dropped the binoculars and realized that he was not alone. Three other neighbors had been watching the lights, too. They all congregated and began to talk about what they had seen.

When George and Edna went inside, they felt exhausted. George was surprised to see that they had lost an hour somehow. He would have sworn that the sighting had taken only minutes.

George was very troubled by what he had seen. He had heard stories of UFO encounters for his entire life, but he had never believed any of them. He had always thought that people who reported UFO sightings were doing so because they were either hysterical or they wanted attention. He was having a difficult time accepting that he had just had a strange sighting.

That night George suffered a terrible nightmare. He dreamt that he was on a hospital bed and someone was just above him. He was pinned down or tied in some way and his head was blocked so that he could barely move it. He couldn't see the figure clearly in the darkness, but he could make out a humanoid shape. The figure forced a long, thin object into his nose. George gasped in pain and startled awake. He sat in bed shaking and sweating. The dream seemed so real! He'd never had such a lifelike dream before.

The next morning Edna awoke complaining of her muscles hurting in her right arm. The arm ached as if she had overused it, but she couldn't remember doing anything that would have hurt it.

In the following weeks George continued to have upsetting dreams night after night. Edna's arm continued to deteriorate. She sought help from her doctor but no one could explain what had happened to the muscles in her arm.

George could not help but think that all his troubles began the night that they saw the lights in the sky. Eventually, he contacted a UFO researcher and asked him to come to the house.

George sat down with the researcher and awkwardly began. "I never believed in UFOs," he said. "I always thought that people who saw them were reporting just so much tomfoolery, but I have to tell you that my wife and I saw something a while back that has changed our lives."

George poured out his entire tale. He gave the names of his neighbors who had also seen the lights take off, and they verified the story. He felt a little better when the researcher seemed to take him seriously. Maybe the researcher couldn't take away the nightmares nor help Edna's arm, but he believed them. The researcher helped the elderly couple understand that they were far from alone. What had happened to them had also happened to many other folks. They were possibly suffering from "missing time." They might have been abducted and tested or experimented on. At least the researcher offered a voice for the dark thoughts that George had been experiencing all along.

George and Edna did continue on. They still suffered from the effects of their experience, but they found a community of loving people willing to help them heal. It was indeed a strange ending to the couple's experience in their Boswell home.

THE BEING IN THE WOODS

For many years, people who experienced UFO or creature sightings had nowhere to go. They feared ridicule and often had no idea who to tell about their encounters. Years later many of them would contact UFO and Bigfoot researchers with their old stories. These were usually sincere people who believed that their experiences needed to be noted, and quite often they were still traumatized long after their encounter. Such is the case in the following story.

It was the spring of 1954 and Helen was dawdling a bit to enjoy the sunshine and fresh air. School was out and she was on her way home from Father Brown's Parochial School near Pittsburgh. Her school uniform felt warm and itchy that sunny afternoon and Helen couldn't wait to be free of it for the summer.

Helen took a shortcut through a thicket of trees as she headed home. It was a familiar path and she moved along comfortably. The trail twisted around and Helen froze as she rounded the turn.

Before her was a small, saucer-shaped craft. It sat squat on the ground as she observed it. The craft was smooth and showed no openings, seams, or marks. The craft was small enough that it couldn't have held more than one or two beings.

After a time, Helen's eyes shifted to a being about six feet from the craft. The figure was humanoid but she felt that it was not human. The proportions were wrong for a person. The being was extremely thin and held itself oddly. Helen studied the figure for about fifteen seconds but it never moved.

Helen stood frozen, too. She had no idea what to do and was afraid that any movement would draw the being's attention.

Without warning, the figure and craft just faded away. It happened quickly and Helen found herself looking around to see if they had moved elsewhere, but there was no sign of either the craft or the being. They had simply disappeared into thin air.

Helen was adamant about what she had seen and even drew a diagram of the ship and the person. Though many years had passed before Helen called Dr. Paul Johnson's team at the Pennsylvania Center for UFO Research, she remained convinced of her strange experience.

INCIDENT AT RED ROCK

The names of the two Air Force technicians involved in this case have never been released, but this story has been circulating since the mid 1960s. The place where the story occurred and all the places around it existed at the time of the events. One of the original sources for this story was a letter from a man claiming to be the brother of one of the techs. That man was former Chief Master Sergeant Walter, whose reputation was impeccable. In the end, it is up to the reader to decide what really happened. However, the story's basic facts have not changed through all of the intervening years.

It was a cold and blustery morning on March 5, 1965, as the two Air Force technicians suited up to go outside. One was a young man named Walter, according to Sergeant Walter's claim. The other technician we'll call Reed. They were stationed at Benton Air Force Station in Red Rock at the border of Sullivan and Luzerne counties. The facility was an air defense center that monitored the air for large-scale bomb attacks on the United States. Large radar antennas were stationed across the country as part of the Aerospace Defense Command Interior Radar Defense Zone. One of the large red-and-white radar antennas was the reason why the two young technicians had suited up. They had to go outside to repair a height-finding radar antenna that was positioned northeast of their location.

Walter and Reed stepped outside and made their way up the mountain to the antenna. They opened their took kits, laid out the tools much like a surgeon would, and began to work. It was a routine operation and they had performed it many times before. Now they worked with practiced ease, but the buffeting winds stinging their skin made them hurry. Pennsylvania in March is rarely a hospitable place.

Suddenly one of the technicians caught sight of motion in the distant sky. A disc-shaped object was high above them, coming in their direction. The technician paused in his work.

"What in the world is that?" he asked aloud.

His partner followed the first technician's gaze and paused, too. They saw the disc-shaped object descending from the sky.

The object settled to the ground not far from where Reed and Walter had been working. Both men were amazed by what they were seeing, and the craft was like nothing they had ever encountered before. Was it something new that the Air Force was using? The men laid down their tools and walked toward the craft for a better look. No doors opened and no pilot was visible. It was very puzzling.

Reed and Walter were only a few feet away when a bright light suddenly shot out of the craft directly at the two young men.

Inside the radar station, the other technicians and Air Force personnel continued to work. They weren't a bit concerned about the two technicians outside. It was just routine work that they were doing and they'd be back soon. But Walter and Reed did not return when they should have.

Walter and Reed never reported back to their command post that day. The Air Police were notified that the men were missing and they hurried out to the work site. They found the tools laid out as if Walter and Reed had been working on the antenna, and then simply walked away.

The Air Police failed to locate Walter and Reed, and so they notified the Pennsylvania State Police. The police began a search of the area that continued for sixteen hours. What had happened to the two young technicians?

Finally, a state trooper driving down Route 487 saw two young men in uniforms walking along the highway. They were staggering and seemed disoriented. The trooper pulled up to the men and saw immediately that they were Reed and Walter. The men were confused, dehydrated, and slightly injured. Both men had strange marks on their necks and they couldn't explain how the marks had gotten there. In fact, the men were unable to answer most of the questions put to them. They did not know how many hours had elapsed, where they had been, or who or what had taken them. All they did know was that they were fixing the antenna when they saw a "small saucer-shaped object" land nearby.

The men were transported to Williamsport Hospital, where they were treated for dehydration. The men were tested for drugs and alcohol but were found to have neither in their systems. Reed and Walter were then transferred to the Air Force hospital at Stewart Air Force Base in New York, where they were examined once more. Other than the marks on their necks, they were fine. Their clothes, however, were covered in trace amounts of alpha radiation that had no natural explanation. The men described what they remembered, but they had no memory of any events after they were shot by the beam of light.

Reed and Walter spent about two weeks in the Air Force hospital being examined both physically and mentally. They were both released back to their unit.

According to Chief Master Sergeant Walter, his brother was questioned at an Air Force Psychiatric Center at Sheppard Air Force Base in Texas in 1966. It was there that a doctor asked Walter if he thought he had been abducted by extraterrestrial visitors. Walter would refuse to speak about the incident at Red Rock after his questioning in Texas.

What happened to Reed and Walter at Red Rock? The truth is that no one really knows. All that is known is that two dependable young Air Force technicians claimed to have seen a saucer-shaped object that shot a bright light at them. They then lost more than sixteen hours of time. They would be found dazed, dehydrated, and bearing strange marks on their necks. The men would be physically and mentally tested and found to be of sound body and mind. Both Walter and Reed would return to duty serving in the United States Air Force, and would refuse to talk about the incident afterward. It is a singular event in Pennsylvania's UFO history, but strangely, the story is virtually unknown.

WHAT HAPPENED TO HENRY

Mary stroked her son's dark hair and watched him as he settled in to sleep. Henry was nine years old and she had thought that he had outgrown many of his childish fears. But now Henry was once again terrified of the dark, of small noises, and of shadows. He had been a normal, healthy nine-year-old until only a few weeks earlier. That was the night when he had first awakened screaming about the bad doctor who had taken him to a spaceship. Ever since that night in 1983, Henry had been a frightened, shaking bundle of nerves.

Mary closed her eyes and leaned against the headboard of the bed. She was exhausted. The past few weeks had been terrible. There had been the nightmares, the personality changes in her son, and the doctors. The school had insisted that she take Henry to a psychologist; he told her that Henry was schizophrenic. Mary and her husband David were physically and emotionally drained.

Henry was hearing voices that others could not hear and seeing people he called "monsters" or "aliens," who he claimed were taking him away to a spaceship. He wept that "the mean doctor" did terrible, painful things to him.

Mary startled awake when David poked his head through the door. "Go to bed, Mary, I'll sleep in here tonight."

Mary stood up gently and looked down at her sleeping son. He was her baby, the youngest of their three children, and her fear for him sat like a lump in her throat.

"He's already sleeping. Come to bed." she whispered.

David nodded and took her hand as they walked down the hallway.

Mary felt herself torn out of her sleep by the keening screams from her son. She stumbled out of bed and heard David scrambling along behind her. The other kids were awake and met Mary in the hallway. Nancy, her eldest, looked bleary-eyed and concerned. "Isn't Henry going to get better soon?" she asked. There was exasperation in her voice and Mary was aware that the two older kids were getting tired of the nightly dramas and the other problems. The stigma of a "crazy" brother would affect the other two children. Mary paused to herd the children out of the hallway.

David pushed past Mary and flipped on the bedroom light. He found Henry on the floor near the windows. He was dirty and shaking. When David touched him, Henry swung at his father. He was lashing out in terror. He didn't even seem to recognize his parents. There were grass stains on the knees of his pajamas and the bottoms of his pajamas were wet from dew. Blood ran out of the boy's nose and his hands were dirty.

David grabbed the child's hands and held him tight. "Henry!" he urged. "It's me—Daddy."

Suddenly Henry stopped struggling and collapsed into his father's arms. "Don't let them take me again," he sobbed. "Don't let them take me to the mean doctor."

David held Henry and Mary took in the child's condition. How did he get grass stains on his clothes? What had caused the bloody nose? Was Henry going out somewhere during his delusions? Was someone molesting him? A dozen terrible questions ran through her mind. Was someone real actually hurting her little boy?

She hushed the other children and put them to bed again. She hurried on numb feet back to the bedroom. David was changing Henry's clothes and wiping his dirty feet. Mary turned back the blankets for Henry to lie down. He was trembling. "Don't let me alone," he pleaded, and Mary hushed him.

"I'll stay with you," she soothed, but Henry shook his head.

"No, I want Daddy. They might beat you up, Mommy." The fear in Henry's voice was tangible.

David patted Henry's shoulder. "I'll stay," he said. "Just let me talk to Mommy first. I'll be in the hall and I'll leave the door open." Fear hooded Henry's eyes but he nodded his assent.

David and Mary stepped out and Mary held on to the dirty, stained pajamas. "David," Mary hissed. "Did you see these? They are wet and there is grass on them. Someone or something had him outside or else he wandered out alone. I'm not sure which is more frightening. One way or the other, something is happening to our little boy. What are we going to do?" Mary fought hard to keep the panic out of her voice.

David shook his head. "I'm not sure what's happening. I'll sleep with him every night and that way no one will come in and bother him." The fear they both felt was worsened by the fact that they were so terribly confused. It was one thing to fight something that you could see and hear, but what did you do with a shadow? Neither one of them were sure what they needed to do.

For the next few nights Henry slept peacefully and David and Mary were hopeful that whatever nightmare their son had faced had gone away. But then one night Mary startled awake to the sound of Henry's terrified screams. She scrambled out of bed, past the other children, and into the room. She saw David on the floor holding Henry and Henry was seemingly fighting with something that none of them could see.

"No, let me go!" he screamed. "I don't want to go back to the bad doctor. No, please!" Henry subsided into tears. David held the child and Mary tried to reassure the other children that this was just another nightmare.

Mary closed the door tightly behind her. Henry ran to her and she cuddled him up on the bed. He was shaking and when she patted his back to soothe him, he cried out.

Mary pulled up Henry's nightshirt and turned him so that she could see his back. She gasped and David cried out, "What the . . . ?"

Across Henry's back were perfectly spaced little bruises. They looked as if they were made by some sort of suctioning machine. In the center of each bruise was a pinpoint of blood, as if something had punctured the child's flesh. Mary and David had never seen anything like it. The gridwork covered most of the child's back.

"Henry," Mary breathed. "How did you get those marks?"

Henry pulled his shirt down and looked up with sad, tired eyes. "The mean doctor. He sends them to get me and then he does tests that hurt me. Please don't make me go again." The tremble in his voice broke Mary's heart.

"Honey, we aren't sending you to this 'doctor.' Who comes to get you?" Mary tried to keep her voice soft and neutral.

Henry shrugged. "The little gray men—maybe they aren't men. They have big eyes and they talk but their mouths don't move. They take me right out through the closed window and then I float into the ship. That's where the mean doctor is."

David turned Henry toward him. "Henry, I was right here tonight. No one was in the room. I would have heard them. It must have been a bad dream."

Henry shook his head in defeat. "They make you sleep, Daddy. I cried but no one can wake up until they are done. I hear them talking in my head and they tell me that it must be done. It's to help them somehow. I don't really understand."

Voices in his head and strange bruises. Mary and David struggled to understand. Was Henry ill? Had he somehow hurt himself? Nothing made any sense and the couple refused to allow their minds to consider the idea of spaceships and alien beings. They had seen such things on television but they weren't really true. Things like that did not happen to kids in Blair County!

Through the following months, Henry's parents dragged him from doctor to doctor. He was physically fine except that he had bruises, cuts, and marks that they couldn't explain. His mental health kept deteriorating daily. Mary finally had to pull Henry out of school and teach him at home. He was terrified of leaving her and getting on the bus. He couldn't cope with the other children or the teachers in school. Loud noises sent him into hiding and he'd occasionally start to talk to people that only he could see and hear. That made matters worse, and Mary could no longer subject him to the cruel comments of the other children. It was hard enough for her other children to cope with having a "crazy" brother, as some kids said.

Henry was diagnosed as schizophrenic, but the doctors changed the diagnosis again and again. Finally they settled on the idea that Henry was suffering from autism. Mary began to read up on the subject and learned that people don't "get" autism, they are born with it. That didn't make any sense to Mary because she knew that he had been a perfectly normal child until he was nine years old.

As the months went by, Mary began to keep a journal of the events for the doctors. She recorded Henry's dreams of being taken to a ship and what was done to him there. She recorded the messages he said the mean doctor and the others gave him. He grew further and further away from her during this time.

After two years, there was no more hope than before. One summer evening Henry was sitting on the deck playing as Mary grilled steaks. David and the other kids were playing in the yard. Suddenly Henry dropped the toy cars he had been holding. "Mommy," he gasped. "The gray men are coming. Look up!"

David seemed to sense something and he began herding the other children toward the house. It was just before dusk and in the fading light he and Mary both scanned the sky. Suddenly, on the mountain across from their home, they saw a large blue light appear. The light hovered over the mountain, and then winked out. On the next mountain over, the light abruptly appeared again.

The other children were gathered just outside the sliding doors watching the light. Henry was stone-still and watching, too. His eyes seemed riveted to the blue light. It began to pulse.

Mary broke away to grab her new video camera from just inside on the dining room table. She grabbed it and pressed the record button. The blue light popped into focus and she zoomed in on it. The light was saucer shaped and it moved rapidly, as if skipping across the sky. Night was swiftly coming on and she hoped that the camera would continue to record in the fading light.

Suddenly Henry turned. "They are going to come close so that you can see them, Mommy." he said.

Mary didn't know what to believe but she kept filming. The blue light slowly slid closer, and then it took off so fast that she could not trail it. She found the light again and began to film once more. This time the light moved slowly toward them. She could see a circular craft of some kind. It wasn't like any plane she had ever seen. It was like the spaceships on television.

Mary kept filming but she also kept Henry close against her side. No one was going to get him away from her. The craft drifted overhead and she tipped her head back to film it better. She held her breath, as if breathing might make it disappear. Suddenly the craft shot off toward the mountains once more and the entire family made a dive for the house as if a spell had been broken.

UFOs! Mary's mind screamed. Until now she had not been sure that what Henry was telling her was true, but here was her proof. It wasn't schizophrenia or anything else—Henry's stories of UFOs were accurate.

At first Mary thought about telling the doctors about the UFOs, but then she began to fear that they'd think she and David were crazy. They talked about it, viewed the footage, and even tried to broach the subject with Henry's doctor, but they found that it wasn't very easy. The doctor was convincing Henry that the whole thing had been a bad dream, and Mary could see improvement in her son. It had been nearly two years since the situation had begun and she was just grateful to see hope on her son's face. She agreed with him when he told her that the UFOs were only nightmares. He took the medicine the doctor prescribed and began to go to school again.

Henry would be forever changed. His ordeal with the UFOs and the "mean doctor" had caused him to have a breakdown and he would suffer from the symptoms of autism for the rest of his life. Only occasionally would Mary allow her mind to wander back to that terrible time so long ago when she had seen the UFO, and when she suspected that Henry was abducted and experimented upon. Perhaps she could have talked herself into believing that they were all bad dreams, but she had kept the notes of what had happened and she had kept the video, too. They were mute testimony to the strange and terrible time when something took her son and changed him from a healthy little boy into a troubled child who struggled to succeed.

INTERRUPTIONS

Shelia sat up in bed and tried to quiet her breathing. It had been the same dream again, one in which she was in the driveway outside her childhood home in Adams County. She and her sister, Sissy, were walking toward the dusty old garage. Shelia was about eight years old and Sissy was a year older. Shelia could feel her sister's hand in hers. It was all very real; it was more like a memory than a dream.

Shelia remembered the sound of the big door swinging open and she saw the dust motes dancing in the sunlight. She could feel panic swelling in her but it was unreasonable. She was not normally afraid of the garage. Why was she afraid today?

Shelia and Sissy stepped into the murky half light and turned. In the corner was an old white cabinet that had a counter at waist height. The door to the cabinet opened itself and Sissy squeezed Shelia's hand. It was a warning not to move and Shelia understood it instinctively. Shelia felt pinned.

The door at the top of the cabinet opened more and the two little girls saw an owl inside. It was large enough that it nearly filled the cabinet. The owl turned toward the girls and Shelia felt her breath catch. The bird had no eyes. Instead, it had large white circles that had black pinwheel designs on them. The pinwheels twirled. Shelia felt a cry building in her throat. At the same time the two little girls turned as one and ran out of the garage. The bird terrified them, and for some reason Shelia connected it to UFOs. It made no sense to her adult mind, but that's what it reminded her of.

The dream stuck with Shelia. A few days later, when she was visiting Sissy's home, she decided to bring up the strange dream. "Hey, Sissy, do you remember the old garage at the home place? I had an odd dream about it the other night. I dreamed that we were little girls again and we were walking into the garage and we were afraid." Shelia let her voice die off and Sissy's face blanched, although Shelia had been careful not to give too much of a clue.

Sissy sat her coffee cup down and raised her gaze to meet Shelia's. "Do you mean the time we sneaked in there and saw the owl with the weird eyes like whirligigs? I hadn't thought of that in years."

Shelia felt her heart thump. It wasn't a dream, it was a shared memory. How could that be?

Sissy shuddered. "Want to hear something strange? I always think of that day when I see UFO stuff on TV. Isn't that weird?"

Through the years, Shelia worked, built her life with her husband, and had other dreams. One night she had the first of what became recurring nightmares. Shelia dreamt that she and her sister were in the basement of their family home. In this dream, Shelia was about seventeen and her sister had to be eighteen. Their mother was with them and they were doing laundry. Suddenly they heard a noise outside and the three women panicked. Shelia felt a terrible fear as they saw something walk by the little basement window. The need to hide overwhelmed the women and Shelia felt her stomach grow tight. They had to get out of sight—now!

Shelia's mother pulled the washing machine out of the little nook it sat in. She hurried the girls forward into the little space. She pushed in, too, and squirmed to get the washer back in place as much as possible. Shelia heard the footsteps on the stairs and knew the creature was approaching. She remembered the panic as she thought, "They're coming for us."

Each time Sheila had the recurring dream she'd awake terrified and sweating. It was a terrible feeling, and eventually she decided to test Sissy with the story. On Shelia's next visit to Sissy she brought up the dream. "Do you remember one night in the basement of the old house? We were down there working on the laundry with Mom. Suddenly something sounded outside and we saw something in the window—do you remember it?"

Sissy sat down and looked at her sister, wide eyed. "I remember that night. I remember when that happened . . . or at least I must have dreamed it too. It seems sort of fuzzy. We knew that something was coming for us. Something we didn't like. Mom pulled the washer out and we all hid down there until it came and went. I can't remember what it was but it was little and scary—I remember that."

That was the second "interruption," as Sheila dubbed the dreams, that she had remembered. How was it possible for Sissy to have shared the same dream experiences as her? Shelia had been careful not to give away any details when talking to Sissy.

One day Shelia was visiting one of her cousins, Linda, when the two women began to talk about something that had happened long ago when they had been about twelve years old. Linda, Shelia, and Sissy were in dresses and they were running through a field away from something. Shelia remembered the sense of panic and the fact that they were running through a culvert away from whatever was chasing them. Shelia recalled falling and cutting her knees. She remembered that sense of panic, and then she remembered nothing until later when she awoke in the muddy culvert. Her leg hurt and the blood had dried on it. It was an odd memory and had a dream-like quality. Linda confirmed that it had been a real experience.

And then there were the strange bruises on Shelia's body. Shelia would awaken on occasion to find bruises on her legs, arms, chest, and thighs. Her husband noticed bruises on her back, too. Shelia never had any recollection of how the bruises had happened. It was unnerving to her because she prided herself on being very self-aware. Somehow, though, she connected the bruises to the disturbing dreams she had been having. Privately, she considered the idea of UFOs and the creatures she had dreamed about, but publicly she hesitated to mention it. Nice housewives from Adams County did not say that they were abducted by aliens.

Shelia gave birth to her first child, a little girl whom she was besotted with and adored. To her relief, nothing unusual occurred after the baby was born. Shelia did not find any bruises on her body and she had no problems. She attributed the strangeness from her past to a few uncomfortable memories. But things changed where her second child, a son, was born.

The strange bruises began to reappear on her skin from time to time. Worse yet were the nights when Shelia felt a horrible fear that the "beings," as she labeled them, had taken her infant son.

Shelia would have certain nights when she'd get to the door of the baby's room and then stop. A terrible dread and certainty suddenly gripped her. The room was silent and dark and she wanted to creep in and check on the baby, but an instinct told her that if she went in and found the crib empty, the creatures would be upset and might not bring back her son. She would always wonder about her strange behavior on those nights. Shelia was a fierce mother and would have fought like crazy if someone tried to abduct her son, but she had a strange reaction to what was happening on those occasions. She would turn around and go to bed. She'd lie down and sleep deeply, knowing that as long as she didn't look in the room, the baby would be brought back.

When Sheila's son was only two, he had a bizarre response to seeing aliens in movies and on television. He would cry and point, becoming nearly inconsolable. "Bad men, bad men!" he screamed. "Hurt!" The child was obviously traumatized by the sight of the gray-skinned aliens on television.

Shelia's best friend since childhood was a woman named Leslie. One day Leslie and Shelia were talking and the conversation turned to UFOs. Leslie told Shelia that sometimes she thought she had been abducted by aliens throughout the years.

"I have these dreams," Leslie confided. "In the dreams I am naked and I'm standing in front of a strange carousel of some sort. It is a revolving set of bathroom cubicles. The commodes are full to overflowing and it stinks horribly. I know that I have to step up on one when it rolls by, and that I'll have to sit on that commode and use it despite that fact that it is full and it stinks. I don't want to but I feel compelled to do it. I step up and I try not to think about what I have to do. I concentrate on the wall of the cubicle. It is done up in blue tiles with a distinctive pattern." Leslie pulled a sheet of paper across the table and drew on it. "The tiles looked like this."

Shelia felt the color drain from her face as Leslie was talking. She, too, had experienced the same dream. At least she had thought it was a dream throughout the years. It was something that she had never told anyone.

Instead of looking at Leslie's design, Shelia grabbed another piece of paper. "I've had that same dream, too. Let me draw the tile design and we'll see if it is the same." she said.

Leslie waited while Shelia drew her design and then the women swapped papers. Both looked in dismay at the design before them. It was the same image. Both women had been dreaming the same dream—down to the design and color of the tiles. Was it just a strange coincidence, or had they shared the same experience through-out the years?

The two women would begin to note each time they had the dream again. Strangely, they would almost always have the "carousel bathroom" dream on the same nights. It was a coincidence that would frighten them.

As the years went by, Shelia would find that her experiences grew fewer and fewer, although her son retained his fear of UFOs and alien creatures. Such stories and movies were banned from her home because of his negative reaction to such things. The mysterious bruises no longer appeared and her children grew up.

One day Sheila's daughter was home from college and came into the bathroom to talk to Shelia while she showered and dressed for the day. Shelia's breasts had been hurting for some reason and her back ached, too. She mentioned her back to her daughter and turned away to dry off.

"Mom," Shelia's daughter cried out. "You have bruises all over your lower back. Did you fall? They're nasty."

Shelia turned to look in the mirror. There were deep purple and red bruises all over her lower back. No wonder it ached! Shelia had not fallen or bumped into anything. She had no idea where the bruises had come from—at least, she had no logical explanation for them. Later that month she was informed by her doctor that she had begun menopause. Was that why the "aliens" had begun to show an interest in her again? Was it because they were following all of the changes in her life?

Shelia has no proof of her experiences other than an abiding conviction that something otherworldly has followed her throughout her lifetime. They began their interest during her childhood and continued to follow her for the rest of her life. It is unnerving and frightening. Shelia doesn't want people to know of her experiences or think of her as an alien abductee, although she believes herself to have been one. She treats her experiences as a terrible secret that she only confides to good friends.

OLIVER LERCH

It was Christmas Eve, 1890, and the Lerch family of Indiana County was hosting a church Christmas party. The minister and twenty other folks from their church were enjoying a wonderful celebration. Mrs. Lerch had covered her best tablecloth with the finest foods from their farm. The other ladies of the church had tried to outdo each other with fine foods, jellies, and sweets. It was a lovely spread.

Twenty-year-old Oliver Lerch was charged with keeping the wood boxes full so that the house remained cheery and warm. He had filled each wood box and was brushing himself off when his mother came to him and asked him to fetch a bucket of water. Oliver walked to the kitchen and picked up the bucket. He figured that he'd take a shortcut through the backyard to the well pump. It had been snowing for hours, adding a thick new layer of snow to the piles already outside. He'd just cut through the yard and wade through the snow rather than go the long way around to the pump.

Oliver let himself out the kitchen door and paused for a second to allow his eyes to adjust to the lesser light. It was still fairly bright outside with the moonlight pooling on the freshly fallen snow. He'd have no trouble seeing to make the hundred-yard journey. He stepped down into the virgin snow and began to cut a path to the well.

Inside the house the Lerch family was bustling about, filling coffee cups and glasses of cider. Suddenly a terrible scream cut through the laughter and conversation. Everyone paused and listened. Again the voice cried out.

"Help me! Mama, Dad, someone help me. Help me!" It was Oliver.

Everyone took off running. Someone grabbed a lantern and another grabbed a coal oil lamp. They tumbled outside onto the partly cleared path. Ahead of them they saw Oliver's footprints in the fresh snow. The bucket lay discarded.

The terrified cries came again. "For God's sake, help me!"

Everyone's eyes turned upward. Above them in the sky was Oliver, struggling as if something held him but they could not see anything above him. Oliver writhed and screamed for help as he slowly levitated upward. His poor family jumped and grabbed at him. Those in the group could do nothing but watch as the young man drifted up into the darkness and away from them forever.

Oliver was never seen nor heard of again, and those who were there that night told the story for years. They all averred that whatever had taken Oliver had lifted him up from the middle of the yard. The tracks in the snow told a terrible and puzzling tale. Who or what had taken Oliver up into the sky?

THE STRANGE STRANGERS

The cool Pike County air greeted Frances Stichler as she stepped out into the predawn darkness to tend to her farm work in May of 1957. This was a peaceful time of day, and Stichler planned her schedule as she walked toward the chicken coop.

A low humming noise caused Frances to pause just outside the barn. What was that sound? She'd never heard anything like it before. She looked upward and froze. Fifteen feet above her barn hovered a strange aircraft about twenty feet in diameter. It was shaped like a bowl inverted over a deep saucer. The craft had a hinge of sorts about four feet long that seemed to allow the top to flip up. She later estimated that the craft was about fifty feet off the ground.

The strange craft hovered at a downward angle so that Frances could see into the glass bubble. She saw a man in a shiny gray suit of some sort. The man was wearing a helmet of the same color. He sat inside the craft and she could see him clearly from the waist up.

Frances described the man as "average size with deep-set eyes and a rather long face." She and the man stared at each other for about a minute before the craft shot upward and curved off into the distance. She heard the whirring noise again, but she had not seen any blades or rotors or other devices on the craft that caused motion. She noticed that there was no movement of air such as a helicopter would have made.

Frances went back into her house disturbed and bemused. What kind of craft was that? Who was that man? A Russian spy? (During the Cold War this would have been a very real fear for someone in her position to have had.)

Since Frances had no proof of her sighting, she decided not to call the authorities. She feared that they'd scoff at her. She did confide the story to a few friends, but that only reinforced the idea that she'd be laughed at. They uniformly asked her what she had been drinking. Frances did not drink.

As bizarre as Frances's story was, investigators could have told her that she was not the only person to have seen such a craft. When Frances finally decided to tell officials about her sighting, UFO researchers were called in. The researchers found that there were other people in the area who reported seeing a similar craft in the days around Frances's sighting. No one else had such a clear view of the driver, though. Frances staunchly maintained that her story was absolutely true despite the lack of physical evidence to support it. No rational explanation was ever offered for this sighting.

The Healing Helpers

Jason laid back in his bed and sighed. He was exhausted and all he had done was get up to go to the bathroom. His wife, Ellen, had to help him up and bear most of his weight as he eased into the wheelchair. Jason felt worthless, hopeless. He had been sick for several months and he saw no end to the illness in sight. In fact, the doctors did not seem to know what was wrong with him. He was weak, his legs felt like rubber, his chest hurt, and he was constantly exhausted. He could barely eat and his whole body ached. Without a diagnosis, Jason was worried that this would never end. What would become of him and his family? How could he earn a living for them if he was ill? They had been living off of their savings and he had used up his sick days and vacation time. Now they were forced to go to the welfare department for help. It made Jason feel useless. Ellen was talking about getting a job again. Jason kept sinking further into despair.

The phone rang and Jason heard Ellen answer it. The conversation on her side revealed little. She kept saying "I see" and "yes" over and over again.

Ellen hung up the phone and stepped inside the bedroom. "Jason, that was the doctor's office. They have finally diagnosed your illness. The doctor says that you are suffering from acute angina. They want us to go back in next week so that they can talk to you about it. Until then you are to rest and stay calm."

Jason absorbed the news. At least there was a reason for what was happening to him. He laid back and closed his eyes to rest. Ellen kissed his forehead and told him that she was going out for a while.

Some time later, Jason startled awake. He had heard a sound. Was it Ellen coming home? The room was filled with dusky shadows. He heard a scurrying noise and looked around. Something was moving in the shadows. Jason wanted to call out for Ellen but he was afraid to make a sound. He was not alone—but who or what was with him?

The shadows shifted again and Jason tried to push himself up but he couldn't move. It was like someone was pinning him down.

Two small figures stepped out of the darkness. They could not have been more than three feet tall. The figures had large heads with black, slanted eyes that were too big for their faces. Jason wanted to scream but no sound left him. Within his head he heard a voice.

"Don't be afraid. We have come to help," it said. Jason felt his muscles relax slightly. The figures came forward and each of them reached out. Jason felt his hands opening and the beings laid little black boxes in them.

The beings spoke again within Jason's head. "Lie still. We are here to help you. Rest."

Jason saw images in his head, including that of a large, circular craft landing at the nearby golf course. Jason realized that the beings were telling him where they had come from. He knew that he should have been terrified, but he wasn't. He felt warmth radiating into his hands from the black boxes.

Jason felt an urge to close his eyes. He was tired but the pain in his chest was lifting. Sleep overtook him.

When Jason awoke again it was morning and Ellen was in the bathroom getting dressed. He could hear her humming and he sat up without thinking about it. There was no pain in his chest. He stood up and his legs easily held his weight. Without thinking about it, he started walking toward the bathroom. He wanted to tell Ellen what had happened to him. Ellen was shocked when Jason opened the bathroom door. "Jason, you're walking?"

He began to pour out his strange tale about the visitors from the evening before. Ellen looked at him in disbelief. "They placed these little boxes in my hands and I could feel warmth from them," he explained. As he spoke, Jason held up his hands. He and Ellen saw the red patches in the palms of both hands. Both were in the perfect outline of the black boxes he had seen.

Ellen looked at Jason in amazement. "What happened to your hands?" she breathed. Jason's gaze met hers and they both knew the answer. Someone or something that they couldn't explain had come to visit Jason the night before. Whoever the beings were, they were not human and they seemed to come for the express purpose of healing Jason. After that, Jason would continue to get better. He made a full recovery without medical intervention—at least without medical intervention of the human kind.

Monsters and UFOs

The idea of aliens is terrifying enough, but there is an entire class of UFO sightings that includes encounters with strange creatures. These creatures range from unusual alien beings to Bigfoot-type beasts and other monsters.

UFO Encounter at Lake Erie

Presque Isle State Park sits on the shores of Lake Erie and is a beautiful place to visit. Hikers, sun worshippers, picnickers, and others come from all around the nation to visit this historic park. On July 31, 1966, sixteen-year-old Betty Jean Klem and her boyfriend, eighteen-year-old Doug Tibbets, decided to have a picnic at Presque Isle Park. They invited some friends, including twenty-two-year-old Anita Haifley, who brought along her two small girls and a friend, twenty-six-year-old Gerald LaBelle. They chose Beach 6 for their picnic site.

By all accounts, it was a beautiful afternoon. The children played and everyone had a lovely time. As dusk settled in, the group began to pack up to go home. They walked through the sand to where they'd parked the car. To their dismay, the wheels of the car were swamped in the sand. They were stuck.

Gerald volunteered to walk out and find help. He told Doug to stay and keep the girls company. The children were tired and were lying down in the car. The two women and Doug got into the car to wait for Gerald's return. He'd surely run into someone or find a park ranger before very long.

Betty Jean watched the darkness descend. It was creepy out on Presque Isle alone at night, she thought. She glanced at her watch. It was 9:30 P.M. and a lazy summer moon lit up the darkness. Betty Jean hoped that Gerald would return soon. Still, the sky was pretty. She admired the twinkling stars. As she studied the heavens, she gradually became aware that something was moving in the sky. One of the stars moved erratically, unlike any falling star she had ever seen. She was curious about the unusual behavior of the celestial object. She pointed it out to the others in the car, and the three adults turned their attention to the strange star. Almost instantaneously they all realized that what they were seeing was not a star but a craft of some sort. The object drew much closer and now they could see that it was mushroom-shaped and metallic looking. It was backlit by lights and it dropped down until it was about three hundred yards away from the car. The witnesses were riveted with fear. The craft shot out beams of light that somehow seemed to help it land.

Unbeknownst to the stranded picnickers, two park rangers were coming up on them from the other side. The lights suddenly winked out and the craft shot off again toward the north. When the park rangers knocked on the window of the stranded car, everyone screamed. They poured out a strange and twisted story to the rangers. The rangers, who had not seen anything, tried to calm them down and tell them that nothing was wrong. The officers agreed to look around in order to reassure the girls. Doug got out of the car and went with the officers.

Betty Jean and Anita locked the car doors and scanned the darkness anxiously. There was something wrong in the area and they were both frightened. Betty Jean caught motion in the darkness and strained to see what it was. The guys had flashlights, but the mysterious object moved as part of the darkness. Betty Jean could not believe what loomed out of the blackness toward her. It was a humanoid creature approximately six feet tall and covered in long black fur. It was walking quickly, swinging its arms, and it seemed intent on getting to the car. Betty Jean screamed and smashed her hand down on the car horn. The beast paused, then reversed course back into the darkness.

The rangers and Doug returned with Gerald and listened to the girl's hysterical story. They decided that she really must have seen something—but that something had to have been a bear.

Betty Jean shook her head. That had not been a bear. She suddenly remembered that she had heard a scraping noise just before she had honked the car horn. The creature had been just outside the car at that time.

The officers flashed their lights along the side of the car where the girl indicated. They froze. Long, gouged claw marks scored the paint. Everyone decided that it was time to get out of there. They freed the car from the sand and left.

The park rangers reported the events to the local police and they sent out officers to examine the area at first light. The officers easily found the area where the car had been stranded. They located an area with strange depressions, like marks made by the legs of an object. Each set of marks was eight feet from the next in a roughly circular patch. But the strangest things the officers found were clear, deep footprints in the sand from the depressions to where the car had been. The footprints were not from human feet, and they were not bear tracks. The beast had left long, sharp claw indentations in the sand.

Gossip spread quickly, and within hours the tale of monsters stalking Presque Isle filled the air. Media picked up on the story. Local park rangers did not want to see tourism suffer in the area and they reiterated their claim of a bear, but Police Chief Dasanio shocked many when he told a press conference that there were no bears out in that area the night of the sighting. The police released information about the strange depressions they had found and made casts of the footprints. Chief Dasanio called in the Air Force. Officers from Wright-Patterson Air Force Base in Dayton, Ohio, were sent. A Major Hall was the lead officer investigating the case. He took impressions of the footprints and the depressions. According to Major Hall, the Secretary of the Air Force would have to release any findings after the study of the casts was completed. With that, the major packed up and left.

Beach 6 was now an even greater local attraction. People were pouring in to view the marks and large groups turned out at night to watch for UFOs. During that time, several people would report seeing strange lights in the sky but the park police and local police would not believe the accounts. However, there were several other witnesses who did not want publicity. They were credible people who were not out UFO hunting. They only told their stories to the police on the promise of anonymity.

One of the most credible subsequent sightings came from the police themselves. Three nights after the initial sighting, two officers reported watching a bright UFO over Lake Erie near Lawrence Park for more than two hours.

The park management realized that the tourist season was in jeopardy. The park superintendent announced that the park was totally safe and that there would be no more talk of UFOs at Presque Isle.

WOLFMAN AND THE UFO

Elsie Wainwright and her husband Alan sat on their back porch near Bensalem looking up at the stars on the night of August 27, 1973. The cool breeze offered them a respite from the hot, sticky summer air. Elsie pressed her iced tea glass against her forehead to further cool herself. Alan was sitting propped back in a lawn chair with his feet up on the banister. Another cool breeze wafted past them as Alan looked at the stars.

Elsie followed his gaze. "It looks like you should be able to reach out and touch them, doesn't it?" she asked.

Alan grunted, and then suddenly he dropped his feet to the floor of the porch. "What the . . . ?" he exclaimed.

Elsie looked back at the sky and gasped. A large, boomerang-shaped craft was moving across the sky. Blue lights outlined it, giving the craft a clearly defined shape. The moon backlit the craft further. It was not like any plane they had ever seen before. The craft stopped moving and hovered in place.

Elsie and Alan were mesmerized. Suddenly the boomerang craft shot forward across the mountains, and then zigzagged back toward Beech Hill. The craft then dropped low below the tree line. The glow of the lights from the craft lit the sky above the hill.

"Did that thing land or did it crash?" Alan asked.

Elsie shook her head. Her voice was a bewildered whisper. "I don't know. I don't even know what it was."

Alan got up and headed for the kitchen door with a purpose. "Where are you going?" Elsie demanded in a panic.

Alan turned back for just a second and she could see the determined look on his face by the light from the kitchen. "I'm going to go see if that thing landed or crashed. Could be someone needs help up there on the hill. Might be some sophisticated new plane the government's working on or something."

"Do you think it's safe?" Elsie asked. "Maybe we should just call the police and let them deal with it."

Alan snorted. "I ain't calling anyone and telling them that I saw some strange airship crash on Beech Hill until I know what's going on up there. I'll just take a look and I'll be right back."

Elsie stood up and headed for the door. Suddenly she didn't want to be outside alone anymore.

Alan came out with his heavy-duty flashlight and his .410 shotgun. He had two pumpkin ball shells in his hand and loaded them into the gun. "Lock the door and wait for me to come back." Alan instructed.

Elsie nodded. She still felt uneasy but she knew it would do no good to voice her concerns. She watched from the kitchen window as Alan set off over the field toward Beech Hill. It was a good fifteen-minute walk but Alan knew the terrain well. As long as he stuck to the path, he'd be fine—or at least she hoped so.

Alan wasn't thinking about UFOs as he flipped on the flashlight and stepped onto the path. He had never put any stock in such foolish tales, but he did believe that the government created some really strange planes for spying on our enemies. He wondered if what they had been seeing was one of those.

Alan walked along the path until he saw the light in the distance. Suddenly he felt the hair on the back of his neck rising. Maybe he was scaring himself, but then again, maybe there was someone out in the woods watching him.

Alan inched forward toward the lights but before he ever got close enough to see the craft, he heard a branch snap behind him. Alan whirled around and came face-to-face with a large figure. It was at least six feet tall and had black, beady eyes that blinked at Alan in the harsh light from the flashlight. He raised the flashlight so the beam of light was fully on the beast's face. Alan froze in shock. The creature's face was doglike and hairy.

The beast stepped toward him and Alan brought his gun up, firing off one shot. The beast ducked out of sight and Alan ran past it back down the path toward the house.

Elsie had heard the single gunshot in the distance, and then she saw the light bobbing along as Alan sprinted in her direction. She unlocked the door and threw it open before he got to it. He dove inside and slammed the door shut. His breathing rasped in his throat and he turned to fumble the locks into place. "Lock the front door, too," he gasped.

Elsie saw Alan's fear and ran to lock the door. Then she returned to find Alan sitting at the table trying to catch his breath; he held the gun in his lap as he watched the back door, as if expecting it to be broken in.

"What happened?" Elsie demanded, but Alan shook his head.

It took nearly half an hour before Alan gave up his vigil at the back door. Then he drank a cup of coffee before he could talk. What he eventually described to Elsie made her sit down, astonished.

The couple would later report the sighting and the wolfman-type creature to investigators. They never wanted their names released and they never made any money from their experience. However, they would maintain that their story was true for the rest of their lives. What did Alan see in the woods? He would never really know, but he suddenly became a believer in UFOs and in creatures from other worlds. It was harder for him to doubt others now because he believed that he had come face-to-face with such a creature that night on Beech Hill.

THE STRANGE THING IN DEBBI'S HOUSE

It was a warm night in August 1984, and Debbi Carson was going home after giving a friend a guitar lesson. Debbi lived in rural Armstrong County and she loved living out in the country. She turned onto the primitive lane that led to her home. It was dark and she had to go slowly to avoid the rocks and potholes. At last Debbi parked the truck and glanced over at her little daughter. The baby was only three months old and was peacefully asleep. It was a shame that she'd have to wake the child, but she needed to get her in the house.

Debbi gently eased her little daughter from the car seat and began to walk up the path to the house. Halfway to the door, she heard a "strange humming sound" in the air above her. At the same time a bright light illuminated the area around Debbi, while her dog began barking and growling. She put a hand over the baby's head and looked up, expecting to see a helicopter. Instead she saw a long craft shaped roughly like a fish. It was cylindrical in front but had a wedge sticking out in the back. The craft had a spotlight on it and it was outlined in lights. There were also lights flashing in the woods nearby. The craft moved off and hovered about twenty-five feet above the ground between two pine trees some distance away in the woods. Debbi realized that the craft couldn't be a helicopter because there was no whirring from rotor blades and not a bit of wind.

As suddenly as the craft had appeared it sped up and shot away. Debbi was left open-mouthed and surprised. What had the craft been?

Debbi went in, placed the baby in the playpen, and ran back outside. She could still hear the humming sound, but now it reminded her of angry bees. She saw the lights blinking in the woods and it spooked her. She grabbed her guitar from the truck and ran over and unhooked the dog. It was still barking furiously at the sky and Debbi pulled it back inside with her and the baby.

Debbi called her mom to tell her what she had seen. Debbi then called a neighbor and inquired if they had seen the lights. She explained what she had witnessed, and then decided to go back out and check on the lights. This time she heard nothing and she began to calm down. She last remembered sitting in the living room in the dark; when she became conscious again two hours had passed. She immediately checked on the baby and found that she was safely asleep in the playpen. Debbi hurried outside to see if the craft or any sign of it was still there. This time there was no sound or lights flashing.

Throughout the following months, Debbi's home would become a center for strange activity. Her neighbors contacted her on several occasions to ask if she was okay. They would report seeing lights flashing in the woods near her home. Even neighbors who did not know about the initial sighting reported seeing the lights.

Debbi also saw the lights on several occasions. Each time it was in the middle of the night, and on at least four separate occasions, she encountered a strange being in her bedroom immediately after seeing the lights. She described the being as human in shape and wearing a motorcycle outfit. He was about five and a half feet tall and had no hair, but he wore a strange, black skullcap with a point that came down over the forehead like a widow's peak. The man had slits for his eyes, nose, and mouth. She reported that the man spoke to her in her head and that he made her feel peaceful.

On one occasion, the figure told her not to be frightened and that he was there to learn about humans from her. He then told her that he'd return again and they could talk more then.

On another visit, he told her that he was there to help everyone. He said that there were things wrong on Earth. He said that Earth people were not doing the right things. He told her that his people always had peace and that Earth people must learn to have peace with each other.

In May 1986, Debbi and a neighbor contacted the Pennsylvania Center for UFO Research and a case was opened. Researchers listened to the information and searched the area for physical evidence. As they went through the story, they noted the time lapse on that first night. Debbi had lost two hours and that became a focus for them. What had happened during those two hours? Debbi had no conscious memory of the missing time and she agreed to be hypnotized in an effort to find the truth.

According to Debbi's testimony under hypnosis, she took the dog out after things had settled at her home. She took the dog for a walk in the field near the house, where the dog began act very oddly. It barked and then whimpered. The dog pulled on its leash and tried to drag her along. The dog was pulling so hard on its leash that it was choking itself, so Debbi freed the dog from its leash and it went barking into the darkness. Debbi thought that it must have seen or sensed something.

Debbi then became aware of a strange ship in the sky. It was shaped like the one she had seen earlier, but now it was lying on its side. The humming sound suddenly filled the air and she felt a faint buzz on her skin. She related it to the feeling of a low-level electrical charge. "It was like I stuck my finger in an electric socket," she said.

At that point Debbi realized that she could not move. A figure dressed in a black motorcycle suit came out of the darkness. The figure had on a black skullcap with a point in the front over its bald head. At about stomach level the man wore a medallion that glowed a soft green. Debbi's eyes were drawn to it and she stared at it intently. She got the feeling that the medallion was some sort of translation device.

She felt extremely peaceful and relaxed. The man appeared legless, seeming to melt into a long cylinder at the waist and hovering about a foot off the ground.

Debbi continued to stare raptly at the green light. The male figure spoke in her head and told her that he was learning from her and that he was scanning her brain. She felt a sense of relaxation and peace and her mind went blank. She couldn't form a thought.

Then a circle of the ship's metal wall whirled open and a bright green beam of light shot out. It encompassed the figure and seemed to pull him inside. The door whirled back closed without leaving a seam. The craft shot upward through the hole in the trees and was gone. The dog came running back, and Debbi grabbed it and walked back to the house. She sat down near where the baby slept and stared at the wall until conscious thought overtook her once more.

Debbi's experiences changed her life, but she was fortunate because they were generally positive. She never suffered abduction, experimentation, or the fear and pain that others have.

THE HUNTER OF UFOS

Dan Hageman is a rather quiet, unassuming man. He is also the director of the Butler Organization for Research of the Unexplained, an organization dedicated to investigating UFO events and other paranormal activity. So what makes a gentle family man dedicate part of his life to investigating UFO activity? Ask Dan, and in his understated way he'll simply answer, "My interest in the UFO phenomena began at a very early age. I was five or six years old when I had my first UFO encounter."

When Dan was a little boy, his family would make weekly Sunday visits to his grandparents' house. Those were wonderful days in the country with aunts, uncles, and cousins all visiting the old family home. On one particular Sunday evening, Dan's uncle Jack was driving Dan's family home. In the car that night was Dan's uncle, his aunt, his mother, and his two sisters. Little Dan was tucked into the front seat between his uncle and his mother. Uncle Jack drove a 1959 Ford

Fairlane Skyliner, with a glass-topped front roof. Dan loved watching the sky as they drove along.

It was dark out and Dan watched the stars flashing by as they made the forty-minute drive along Route 38. They were only about seven miles from home near the Oneida Valley Dam when Dan first saw the "funny lights." The two lights were orange-colored discs that glowed a soft golden yellow. The discs were keeping pace with the car, which was traveling at about fifty miles an hour.

Dan's mom leaned over and cuddled him. "You're being very quiet tonight. What are you doing?"

Dan looked up and pointed at the glass ceiling. "I'm watching the funny lights." Dan's mother looked up and everyone else's eyes went upward, too.

Uncle Jack glanced up, and then flipped off the car lights to see if the discs were reflections from the bright dashboard lights. The little orange discs still kept pace with them in the sky. Uncle Jack turned the lights back on.

Dan's mom was watching the lights curiously. "Jack, what do you think that they are?"

Jack shrugged. "I have no idea."

Jack saw a wide spot along the road and signaled to pull over. He turned off the car and opened the door. Without the car lights and the engine sounds, they were better able to observe the lights.

The lights seemed to sense that the car had stopped and they paused up in the sky. The lights were growing larger, as if they were getting closer. They were now about six times the size they had first been. Dan would describe them as "dinner plate" size. Now Jack was looking directly at the lights, and the rest of the family was following them through the glass car roof.

Jack stared intently at the lights. They began to rotate in opposite directions and Jack leaned back down. "I don't hear a sound," he told those in the car before straightening up to follow the lights once more.

Suddenly, Jack slid back into the car and started it up. With squealing tires and a spray of gravel, he sent the car careening forward. Jack straightened out the car and looked upward. The objects were moving again and keeping pace. Without warning, Jack slammed on the brakes as he hit a curve. The objects matched the car's speed as Uncle Jack slowed and sped up as the road allowed.

Inside the car there was some confusion. Dan's mother kept asking, "What is it? What are they, Jack?" In the backseat Dan's aunt was trying to keep the girls calm.

Uncle Jack kept glancing up as he tried to follow the road at what seemed to young Dan like a terribly fast speed. "I don't know," he told his sister, "I just don't know."

The objects suddenly disappeared when the family was about a mile from their home in Butler. The family discussed what they had just witnessed for the short remainder of their journey. Inside the house, the children were hustled off to bed. Dan remembered hearing the grownups talking in the next room. What had they seen?

In the following days, there was a lot of talk about the issue in the Hageman household. The local paper declared the next morning that strange lights had been seen in the northern sky above Butler the night before. There had been several reports of the lights.

If this had been the only sighting for young Dan, he would probably have forgotten the lights—but it would not be his only sighting. When he was seven years old, he once again saw the lights.

On a warm summer evening in 1959, Dan was playing on the porch while his mother was in the house bathing. She had cautioned him not to disturb her. Dan glanced up at the early evening sky and froze. There were lights in the sky swinging back and forth, in and out of the cloud bank. Dan watched the lights for some time. He remembered his uncle's experience and listened for sound, but there was none. The lights moved rapidly, and eventually he decided to go get his mother. He was not upset in any way but he thought that his mother might want to see it.

Dan's mom wasn't interested in "what he saw" and told him not to bother her while she was bathing. Dan went back outside but the lights were gone. By the time his mother came out for him, there was nothing to see and he brushed off the event without telling her about it.

About a week later, Dan's mother had a terrible headache. It was after dark and she had put the children to bed. Dan remembered that she had told him to go to sleep, but he wasn't tired. He heard his mother moving around in the living room as she tried to get comfortable on the couch. Dan got up and peeked out of his cracked door.

While Dan was checking out the area, Mrs. Hageman closed her eyes and tried to relax in hopes that the headache would go away. She had turned off the lights because they hurt her eyes. The sound of the television had been painful, too, and so she had shut it off as well. As she closed her eyes, she caught a flash of white. She opened her eyes to see that the hallway was brightly lit. Mrs. Hageman tried to sit up but she found that she could barely move. It was as if something was trying to pin her.

Mrs. Hageman struggled to sit up. She held her chest and placed her other hand on her forehead. She tried to make a noise but no sound came out. She could not move further. She was stuck on the edge of the couch looking into the hall at the light that had no source. The light grew painfully bright and she squinted. It was then that she became aware of a figure in the light. The figure stepped forward. It was nearly nine feet tall and it was coming up the hallway stairs. At the top of the steps it turned and approached her.

Mrs. Hageman would remember nothing more until morning. She awoke with a headache and it was daylight. She frantically looked around for the figure but saw nothing. She could move easily now and she ran for the phone. She called her brother Jack and begged him to come over and stay with her and the children. Jack tried to calm her and told her that he couldn't because he had to stay home due to his work schedule.

That night Dan's mother was frantic. She tried to feign calm as she put the children to bed. However, she had every light in the house on and the children found it hard to sleep. Mrs. Hageman was herself afraid to fall asleep. She sat on the couch waiting and fighting off the fatigue that threatened to overtake her.

There was a sound from the hallway and Mrs. Hageman turned around to face the noise. She felt her body being pinned once more and knew before she tried that she was not going to be able to move. A scream built in her throat but she couldn't move enough to release it. A figure that was the same size and height as the earlier visitor came up the steps once more, but this time the figure was a solid black shadow. She could see no features, no eyes.

Once again she remembered nothing more until daylight. She was traumatized by whatever had happened during the night, and to this day Mrs. Hageman has been unable to discuss her experience. It has been more than thirty years since the events of that night, and she still cannot remember or face what happened. That was the last time she ever saw the figure—at least, it is the last time that she consciously remembers seeing the figure. And young Dan witnessed the visitations from his bedroom.

Through the years, UFOs became part of the fabric of Dan's life. In April 1982, a now-adult Dan would witness a triangular-shaped craft in the woods near his home off Route 38. He was not alone for this sighting; a friend and his friend's wife would also see the craft.

On that day Dan had taken his friend Howard out to see the work that he'd done on a vehicle he was repairing. Howard's wife had tagged along. As Dan stepped off the porch, Howard grabbed his arm and pointed in alarm at the woods near the house. "What's that?" he demanded.

Dan looked up to see a milky, blue-white, bubble-shaped craft hovering near the garage. The craft was brightly lit and remained there for some time. They could see a metal structure inside the bubble. The craft was only about ten feet above the tree line, and they all stood and watched it for a moment. Dan later described it as so bright that it blinded them.

As if there was some signal, the three of them broke and ran for the house. Inside the house they immediately saw that something was very wrong. The television was flashing a strobe of colors and the lights seemed to surge brightly and then wane repeatedly.

Dan grabbed a set of binoculars and Howard made a dive for a telescope that Dan kept set up for watching the night sky. The binoculars broke and the telescope could not seem to get focused, so the two men then stopped and watched the craft with their naked eyes. The metal craft inside the bubble was triangular with rounded corners. On each end there was a pod with a light that pulsed a bright yellow-white.

They could barely grasp what they were seeing. They saw a mass within the craft that looked like glitter before it evaporated. The craft moved closer, then stopped near the house and a crescent-shaped opening appeared. They saw spheres inside the larger bubble.

Two spheres dropped out of the craft and shot up and down. The right sphere spun around and made a hissing sound. Sparks flew from it. The other sphere did the same, and then they each shot off in different directions. The main craft rocketed upward and disappeared. Dan and Howard heard no sound during that time, other than the hissing from the small spheres.

When Dan told his mother about the event, she gasped. She rummaged around until she pulled out a newspaper clipping. It was about two policemen in New Castle who had seen a UFO hovering over the one officer's home the same evening Dan and Howard had seen the strange bubble craft. The men supposedly watched it, chased the strange craft, and lost it when it crossed the Ohio border.

Throughout the years, Dan has also come to realize that there is time that he cannot account for. He will not say that he was abducted, though.

Perhaps one of the most dramatic events of Dan's life occurred one evening when he looked out the window and was startled to see headlights in the trees, sweeping past his window. All that night he watched the lights as they flashed by. He felt the need to keep his family safe and kept going to check on them. He paced, terrified, and just kept waiting as if he knew that something was about to happen. Dan finally settled on the couch and stayed there until daylight. At first light, he suddenly felt relaxed and fell asleep.

A few hours later his wife woke him, but Dan couldn't explain what had happened to him. He saw nothing to be afraid of, but he had been terrified that night. The next night he fell asleep but suddenly awoke "feeling threatened" and got up. Dan paced, feeling angry and upset. Normally Dan was a mellow man, but he could not shake that feeling.

Eventually, Dan began to suffer from night terrors. He dreamed of spinning, seeing lights, and fighting with something. He would awaken shaking and covered in sweat. The dreams were like none he had ever had before.

As time progressed, so did the dreams. Dan began having nightmares in which he was lying naked on a slanted table and he couldn't get up. He could see blinking control panels and he saw humanoid beings in what appeared to be jumpsuits watching him and holding him down. The sight of them filled him with terror and he began to struggle, but he couldn't get free. Instead, he screamed for help and begged them to let him up. At some point, Dan would awaken; he lay gasping in bed as fear clutched him. The dreams were so real—could they be more than dreams? He barely dared to even think of the possibility.

One day Dan went to a paranormal event and there he was introduced to an older woman who claimed to be a psychic. She reached out to shake his hand; as their hands touched, Dan felt an electrical current go through him. The woman looked at him in shock. "You've been taken twenty-three times," she whispered, holding his hand and looking at him intently.

Since then there have been other strange events. Dan had his knees replaced to ease some pain. One morning after the surgery, his wife noticed that he had "scoop marks" on the back of his thighs. They contacted the surgeon and he confirmed that the "scoop marks" were not there before the surgery, and they were not made during the surgery. Strangely, the marks never did hurt him.

Dan is a shy man who doesn't want to overstate the situation. He won't claim outright that he was abducted. He has more questions than answers, and that is why he researches the subject. He is looking for answers for himself and for others, and he wants to know the truth—the truth that will explain what he has lived through. That is why a family man like Dan dedicates time to UFO research; he must, so that he can protect himself and his family, if possible, from what he has experienced.

JESSUP~AREA ENCOUNTER

Sixteen-year-old Frank shifted his jacket and shivered. It was about 9:30 P.M. on a Friday night in September 1970. Behind Frank were the lights and noise of the Friday night football game. It hadn't been a great game and he had decided to take off early. He was enjoying the crisp night air and the solitude of walking home alone.

As the noise and lights of the football field were left behind, Frank paused to gaze upward. He felt like the only person on the planet. Most of the houses were dark, as the people of the little town of Jessup were at the football game. There were no cars moving along the street and only the glow from the streetlights broke the darkness.

Frank was only about three blocks from home when he saw the most amazing sight of his young life. A large silver disc came into view. Frank froze, staring in awe. What was the thing?

The craft was nearly a thousand feet around and glowed bright white. From Frank's vantage point below the craft, he could see three smaller discs beneath the large silver sphere. Atop the craft there was a turret ringed by lit windows. Frank didn't know what to do, so he simply stood watching as the craft moved from west to east. He was puzzled by the gliding movement of the craft, and by the fact that it made no sound. He watched it for several minutes before he broke and ran for home.

Frank found his parents in the living room and poured out his story to them. He was agitated and begged them to call the police. He had to let someone know what he had seen. Visions of old science fiction movies danced in his head. He had enjoyed a few of them through the years, but never imagined that he'd be living in one. In fact, he had never been particularly interested in UFOs, extraterrestrials, and science fiction.

Frank's parents cautioned him to calm down and be logical. He really didn't know what he had seen, and there was no sense getting everyone excited about what could be just a mistaken identification. After all, Frank didn't want to get a reputation as a crackpot. His parents didn't want folks to make fun of the family. Frank argued that people would believe him. Hadn't the local police officer reported seeing a UFO over Lake Scranton only a few months earlier? The newspapers in the area had reported other sightings throughout the summer of that year. Frustrated and angry, Frank argued with his parents but to no avail. He finally agreed to wait until the next day and they would talk about it more then.

Frank paced around his bedroom. He was angry, frightened, and confused. He walked to his window and froze for a second. Then he closed his curtains and dropped down so that no one could see him. He inched toward the window and poked his head up cautiously so that he could look out once again. Outside under a street light was a strange-looking black limousine. Frank studied the car and its occupants. The street light illuminated the car so that he could see the people inside clearly. There were four men in the car and they were wearing antiquated black clothing. Judging from the fedoras on their heads, they were dressed in clothing from the 1940s. The men sat staring straight ahead. They never moved or glanced at the house, but Frank felt that they were there because of him and what he had seen. He studied the car but could not recognize its make and model. There were no identifying marks or emblems on the vehicle.

Frank had never heard of the "men in black" or the mysterious figures who sometimes visited those who had experienced a UFO sighting. Frank would later write of his encounter that he had not experienced missing time nor had he been abducted. "No verbal or physical contact was made," he noted.

When Frank went to bed that night, the car still sat beneath the streetlights and the men had not yet moved. The next day Frank was glad to see that the strange car was no longer there. He went to school and was surprised when he began to tell his story to his three closest friends. They told him that they, too, had seen something large over the football field, but that the bright lights of the stadium had made it difficult to identify the large, glowing object. The school was abuzz with stories of the object that had passed over the field.

That night Frank had made up his mind to contact the local authorities, but when he looked outside his window he froze. The black car was back and so were the four oddly dressed men. For several nights Frank would find the men across the street as if they were keeping a vigil of some sort. No one else commented about them or seemed to notice them.

Eventually Frank would contact the United States Air Force and the National Investigative Committee on Aerial Phenomenon (NICAP). Neither organization would ever give Frank any of the answers that he was looking for. Frank would write about his experience and post an incident report years later on the Internet. He is still looking for an explanation. What did he see that long-ago night? Who were the four men in strange black clothes who had been posted across the street from his home for several nights? Frank has no answer, but he does have a conviction that something very strange and possibly unworldly happened to him that fall night in 1970.

UFO Flaps

U fologists look for patterns in sightings. These patterns are often referred to as "flaps," and they usually entail multiple sightings in a short period of time. Pennsylvania has had several such occurrences throughout the years.

Mount Union Besieged

Mount Union is a little town in Huntingdon County. It is not known for UFO sightings, but from 1980 to 1981 there were several sightings in that area. The first one was originally written off as a hoax. It involved a strange orange craft reported by Mr. and Mrs. Paul Veitch. The object looked like a triangle with three lights at each point. However, upon inspection with binoculars, it was noted that the entire thing was connected by dowel-type rods. This was a popular trick of the time known as a "candle balloon hoax."

If that had been the only sighting, it would have simply passed. But five nights later a woman named Lois Turner called the police to report a strange sighting of her own. She claimed that she'd stepped outside to see if it had stopped snowing, and there she'd seen two bright "headlights" in the sky. The lights were orange and nearly blinded her, but when they quickly winked out she could see a craft gliding about 120 feet off the ground. The craft made no sound. She described it as "resembling two bowls inverted upon one another, and about as large as two average-size rooms, with a height of six feet in the middle. There were two fin-like projections attached to the top bowl . . . approximately three feet in length. The object also contained four rectangular windows illuminated from the interior by what resembled incandescent lighting."

The craft floated down to the ground and hovered about a foot from the earth before taking off. It rose slightly and headed toward a cemetery. The craft appeared to be about to crash into a house before it rapidly shot upward. It flew into some trees but passed through them without any damage to either the trees or the craft. It just disappeared without a sound, leaving no physical proof of its existence.

Turner called the police and they referred her to the Pennsylvania Center for UFO Research and Dr. Paul Johnson. Later, Turner would learn that the police and local newspapers were contacted by several people who had seen a similar craft that night.

The following year the Veitch family would again have an encounter. On the night in question, several members of the family observed a large, brilliant orange sphere zipping across the sky. At first they thought it was a shooting star, but then it got closer and they realized that it "glowed within itself" and made no sound. It maneuvered over a house and hovered there for approximately four minutes, and then it was simply gone.

During that time there were other reports of strange craft in the area. There was never any explanation for what folks in Mount Union encountered during that year.

The Amberson Mountain UFO Flap

Path Valley in Franklin County is a rural area and not prone to much foolishness. It is peopled with good, hard-working folks who usually go about their business without much fuss, but on the evening of Monday, March 11, 1966, that all changed for some residents.

The Lakeview Motel and Restaurant is located in Fannettsburg and is a local hangout. Some folks leaving the restaurant just after dark that evening noticed a strange disc in the sky. The lights around the disc were blinking white, blue, and pink. The UFO cruised by the little establishment and several people saw it.

The local police were notified, but there was really nothing for them to see when they got there. The UFO had flown the coop. Only a group of very upset people were there telling their stories.

By morning, the gossip mill had begun. Folks firmly took up sides. Some believed that the stories were true, while others said that it was all a lot of hogwash. Things like UFOs just don't visit little towns like Fannettsburg. The sage among the town's populace declared that whatever it was, it was certainly gone now.

Conventional wisdom is not always right. The next night, Tuesday, March 12, was a busy one for UFO investigators. On that night the UFO was sighted in three different villages: Spring Run, Willow Hill, and Dry Run, along the Pennsylvania Turnpike in the Amberson Valley.

The story spread and most people were shaking their heads. The idea of UFOs in Amberson Valley was simply ridiculous. The incident probably had not really happened at all and it certainly would never happen again.

But the reports did continue to trickle in. Night after night the UFO made its appearance. One of the most compelling sightings was reported by a Ms. McGarvey who lived in Chambersburg. She was looking through her binoculars at a strange light that she originally took to be a bright planet. However, the light began to swing and sway and shoot around. Planets certainly could not do that. The object shot out of sight to the east and then returned. McGarvey would later say that "it was flashing red and green lights." She watched the display for over an hour in total.

Now no one wanted to make any predictions about the UFO. The local media had picked up the story. The day after McGarvey's sighting, WMIX-FM radio morning show hosts Lisa Harding and Rick Alexander discussed the subject and took several calls from excited listeners. Alexander expressed his skepticism over the idea of UFOs in general, but he was intrigued by the stories. On Thursday night, March 14, he decided to take a ride to Amberson Mountain just to look around. He was only there for a few minutes before he saw something that changed his mind about UFOs. "It was spherical in nature and had spider-like legs. Occasionally it would flash different lights," Alexander said. It was approximately 7:15 P.M. when he had his sighting.

The last known sighting of the lights was March 16, Saturday night. A Mr. Clayton saw a lighted object at 9:30 P.M. above Amberson Valley. He later told the press, "It looked quite a bit larger than an airplane."

During the flap, *The (Waynesboro) Record Herald Shopper Express*, the *Chambersburg Public Opinion*, and WMIX-FM radio all carried stories about the sightings. No one has ever offered up a rational explanation of what happened that week in Amberson Valley.

Bucks County Under Siege

The year 2008 was a pivotal one in Pennsylvania UFO circles. It was the year of the "Bucks County Flap." In that time, the Mutual UFO Network (MUFON) received 138 UFO reports from around the state, 77 of which came from Bucks County. The reports came from business owners, housewives, respected citizens, and young people. Some folks believed that the reports were because of secret military devices being flown over the area, and others believed that intelligent life from elsewhere was checking out Bucks County. But no one could deny that something unusual was occurring in the county.

The flap officially began on January 27 when 911 received calls that a large "octopus-like" craft was hovering over a Don Pablo's restaurant near Langhorne, Bucks County. Officially, nothing was found.

About 11 P.M. that night an off-duty pizza delivery man on Dunbury Road near Fairless Hills saw a strange craft with blinking white, red, and green lights. He would testify that he saw a strange "something" over the woods near Vermillion Hills. "It was a plane that was flying toward us . . . but the funny thing was, after we realized it was a plane flying next to a distant star we no longer had our sights on the plane, it was the star that appeared to be blinking."

On the evening of April 20, a woman awoke to her dog barking furiously. She laid still and listened, trying to figure out what had upset her dog. She heard a curious sound, something like window screen ripping. The woman got up and padded through the house looking for something out of place while the little dog growled and yipped. She went to the sliding glass doors and opened them so that the dog could go out. While she stood there waiting, she began looking around, and that was when she saw the ship up in the sky. It was hovering over the yard and she slammed the door shut, leaving the dog out in the yard. The witness later wrote, "It frightened me. I shut the door and left the dog outside. I thought I would be sucked up, that's how believable this thing was." The craft began to swing back and forth in the sky in a way that no plane could move. There were lights on the craft that created a cone of light from the craft onto the ground, and then it was just gone.

On April 23, folks at a baseball game in Newtown saw "an orange fireball" streaking across the sky. No explanation was found.

Folks shopping at the Target in Langhorne were shocked to see a large "egg-shaped" UFO flying overhead. Reports indicated that the UFO was white and that it hovered before dropping straight downward out of the clouds. Then it took off, streaking through the sky.

Throughout the summer the sightings continued. UFOs were seen at the Oxford Valley Mall in Langhorne, on the Bristol Pike, and elsewhere throughout the county. They were reported by housewives, businessmen, shoppers, and even police officers. They varied in shape and size, including an amorphous black object reported by police officers, shifting shapes, a boomerang, an egg shape, a bright star, and a glowing ball of various colors. The sightings happened over and over again. The area news covered the story and people continued to look upward for strange craft.

On July 10 a new phenomenon was reported. An unusual craft covered the area of the sighting with "fairy dust." No one identified the strange material.

There were dozens of sightings that summer. Some of the craft were accompanied by other objects and odd planes. One of the favorite places for the UFO to appear was the Oxford Valley Mall. There were several sightings there, and a mysterious letter surfaced claiming that there had been strange airplane activity over the mall during the same period. There were reports of flaming trees and fairy dust sprinkled over sighting locations. Before it ended, there were more than one hundred reports from Bucks County and the surrounding area. Discovery Channel and History Channel went to Bucks County to shoot documentaries about the phenomena.

So what did happen in Bucks County? Skeptics claim that it was simply overactive imaginations or experimental military equipment that was seen. Those who observed the UFOs insist that such mundane answers could not explain what they witnessed. They insist that there is no earthly technology that could create aircraft that moved like those they witnessed. Perhaps, as someone suggested, it was a test by the aliens to see how humans would react to the knowledge that they do exist. If so, then we must have failed, because they left without confirming their presence.

THE KISKI UFO FLAP OF 1984

The Kiskiminetas River, running through western Pennsylvania, creates a rough boundary between Westmoreland and Armstrong Counties. The river valley is noted for its rugged territory and great beauty, but in 1984 the Kiski Valley earned a reputation for something else— UFO sightings.

The first known sighting in the Kiski Valley Flap happened in mid-June of that year. A resident of Leechburg noticed an oblong craft the "size of an aircraft carrier" hovering less than twenty-five yards above the river. The sighting seemed to be a singular event until mid-August.

On August 20, Officer Joseph Caporali of the local police force noted a strange object over the town of Vandergrift. It was almost midnight when he first observed the craft. He pulled over and watched the strange object. It was large and square shaped, like a floating box or building. Caporali would report that the ship opened up and two smaller lighted craft exited it. They circled the larger square craft.

At approximately the same time a citizen of Vandergrift, Bill Ziegmond, pulled up and observed the object alongside the police officer. They began to watch the craft with a set of binoculars. Ziegmond would later say that the object was a perfect square sporting two green and two red strobe lights on the corners. It was solid enough to obscure the stars as it passed before them. They watched as the two smaller ships docked inside the primary craft. At that moment, the police officer clicked on a spotlight and the craft suddenly shot forward "at a fantastic rate of speed."

It was later revealed that forty minutes earlier, a resident of Washington Township, Lori Powell, had called the police to report a "square-shaped object" that flitted through the sky without a single sound.

In the following days, there would be many reports of a large UFO over western Pennsylvania. A woman from the little town of Apollo reported twice seeing a large, square craft along Route 66.

In total, there would be more than forty sightings of the craft in the area. The last known sighting was on September 3, when two men were driving between New Kensington and Vandergrift on Route 56 at about 12:35 A.M. They reported seeing a triangular craft in the sky. They pulled over and observed it moving along as it produced a low humming sound. The craft had a blue light in the center of it and they watched it until it disappeared over a nearby hilltop.

What the strange square craft was, and why there would be multiple craft in the area for several months, are questions that will probably never be answered. At the time, UFO sightings were often unreported for fear of ridicule. Surely the fact that forty different people came forward with their stories indicates that something very strange visited the Kiski Valley that summer.

THE CORRY MINI~FLAP

On the evening of August 21, 1988, a young man in Walltown was surprised to see a large orange-colored burst in the sky. It was about 8:15 P.M. when he observed the burst of light and the trail of white smoke that followed it. The man, who had been a munitions handler in the military, heard no sound at all. At the same time, a person driving on I-80 near Dubois saw the same orange burst. They would both report what they had seen. When it was suggested to the former military man that what he had witnessed was a flare, he was adamant that he knew what that would look like because of his work with munitions and that the object was *not* a flair.

Five nights later, four young adults were driving along Route 426 in Warren County near Spring Creek when they saw two bright white lights floating about a quarter mile away. The lights moved in a pattern as if they were scanning the ground. The young folks pulled over to watch and reported that the lights never moved from the area and the craft made no sound. The four witnesses decided to leave because something about the situation frightened them.

To the young people's shock, the two lights merged into one and took up a position directly behind their car. It seemed to be chasing them as they gunned their Chevy. The light stayed with them as they tried to speed away. It would hurry to within five hundred feet of the car, and then fall behind again.

The driver of the car noticed that every time the light got close to the Chevy, the dash indicators lit up and the temperature gauge rose into the overheat range. When the light backed off, the temperature immediately lowered. Now they were afraid that the car would overheat with the light chasing them, although they did not smell the engine heating up.

The driver saw the sign for the little town of Corry and turned there. They knew the town well and pulled over at the steel mill as the light skipped away from them toward the north. It simply kept moving until they could no longer see it. The young people were rattled by their experience.

Later that night two police officers also encountered a strange light. It was 10:30 P.M. and they were parked in Spring Creek Township looking for poachers. They first caught sight of a bright white light coming toward them from a low altitude. It swung back and forth. They observed the light for several minutes before it disappeared.

On August 27, a little boy from Corry called the Pennsylvania Center for UFO Research to report that he and a friend had seen a circle of light drop out of the sky. It hovered and swung around for several minutes before it left. They did not see a craft nor did they hear any sound. The light, however, shot up at a terrific speed. There had to be something creating that light.

Throughout the month of August, the reports of a strange light sweeping the ground and moving at tremendous speeds continued. The last known sighting was on August 30 in Allegheny County. On that evening, a woman saw a large craft in the sky at about 8:30 P.M. The craft was circular and it glowed a pale pink. The woman reported that it was much larger than a plane. She yelled for her husband and he came out and also saw the craft. They would say that a "pancake-shaped" white light glowed in the middle and was surrounded by about twenty little lights around the edges of the craft. They watched it as it disappeared into the distance.

And with that glowing pink craft, the Corry UFO Flap moved into history. The same questions always apply. Why? What were they looking for? Why did they leave? The problem with UFO sightings is that they leave very little evidence behind, but they nearly always leave the witnesses bewildered and changed.

Bibliography

Books and Articles

Barnhart, Roger. "Out of this World: Butler County a Hotbed of UFO Phenomena." *Butler Eagle*, November 7, 1993.

Crain, T. Scott. "UFO Lifting Power." *The MUFON UFO Journal* 210 (October 1985).

Good, Timothy. *Need to Know: UFOs, the Military, and Intelligence*. New York: Pegasus, 2007.

Hobday, Lance A. *Supposedly True Stories of UFO Sightings*. Self-published, 2009.

Johnson, Paul G. *The Researcher* 5, no. 2 (April 1983).

———. *The Researcher* 6, no. 3 (Summer 1985).

———. *The Researcher* 7, no. 1 (Spring 1986).

———. *The Researcher* 7, no. 2 (Winter 1987).

———. *The Researcher* 8, no. 3 (Fall 1988).

———. *The Researcher* 9, no. 1 (Spring 1989).

———. *The UFO Researcher* (Fall 1984).

———. *The UFO Researcher* (Summer 1985).

Kecksburg: The Untold Story. Directed by Stan Gordon. Greensburg, PA: Stan Gordon Productions, 2004. DVD, 92 minutes.

Ketchman, Vic, Jr. "Eyewitnesses Sight Creature in District." *Irwin Standard Observer*, August 17, 1973.

Lyman, Robert R., Sr. *Forbidden Land: Strange Events in the Black Forest*. Vol. 1. Coudersport, PA: Leader Publishing, 1971.

Moylan, B. Tom. "UFO Witnesses Stick to the Original Stories." *Carbondale News*, November 14, 1974.

Rodeghier, Mark. "UFO Reports Involving Vehicle Interference." *The UFO Register* 5 (1974): 56.

Ventry, John. "More UFOs over Western Pennsylvania." *MUFON UFO Journal* (2008).

Wilson, Patty A. *Totally Bizarre Pennsylvania.* Roaring Spring, PA: Piney Creek Press, 2008.

Online Sources

http://alienufoparanormal.aliencasebook.com/2008/07/02/ufo-sightings-in -bucks-county-pennsylvania—in-the-news—video.aspx

http://www.boru-ufo.com/Sightings_Log.html

http://cbs3.com/local/Bucks.County.UFO.2.762646.html

http://www.city-data.com/forum/pensylvania/6913-benton-pa-2.html

http://www.earthfiles.com

http://www.fas.org/nuke/guide/usa/airdef/sage.htm

http://itouchmap.com/?s=PA&f=military

http://www.metro.us/us/article/2009/03/16/02/4205-85/index.xml

http://www.mufon.com/mufonreports.htm

http://www.nationalufocenter.com

http://naturalplane.blogspot.com/2008/08/bucks-county-pa-ufo-sightings -continue.html

http://www.nicap.org/waves/1970fullrep.htm

http://www.nicap.org/waves/1973fullrep.htm

http://www.nuforc.com

http://www.nuforce.org/CB020824.html

http://www.nuforc.org/webreport/024/S24698.html

http://www.pressenterpriseonline.com

http://www.rense.com/general29/etab.htm

http://www.rense.com/general/30/mystt.htm

http://www.rense.com/general31/filers110502.htm

http://www.rense.com/ufo2/pa.htm www.rense.com/ufo2/pa.htm

http://www.theblackvault.com/encyclopedia/documents/MUFON/ Journals/1985/October_1985.pdf

http://www.theblackvault.com/wiki/index.php/Tyrone,_Pennsylvania _(10-20-2002)

http://theparanormalpastor.blogspot.com/2008/07/ufo-flap-over-bucks -county-pennsylvania.html

http://www.ufocasebook.com/91402.html

http://www.ufocasebook.com/tyronepa2002.html

http://www.ufocenter.com

http://www.ufocrashes.com/carbondale/

http://www.ufocrashes.com/carbondale/archive/barry.pdf

http://www.ufocrashes.com/carbondale/archive/palko_1999_11.1.pdf

http://www.ufocrashes.com/carbondale/eye.html
http://www.ufoevidence.org/topics/vehicleinterference.htm
http://www.ufoevolution.com/forums/calendar.php?do=getinfo&day=2019
   -4-15&c=1
http://www.ufoillinois.com/outofstate/r1970_0925_jessup_pennsylvania
   .html
http://www.ufoinfo.com/filter/1999/ff9936.shtml
http://www.ufoinfo.com/roundup/v07/rnd0738.shtml
http://www.ufocasebook.com/Kecksburg.html
http://www.ufoevidence.org/documents/doc1307.htm
http://www.ufoevidence.org/documents/doc1315.htm
http://www.ufovillage.com/uufoencounters/2008/04212008.shtum
http://www.unknowncountry.com
http://wjz.com/watercooler/ufo.bucks.county.2.915245.html

Archives

Dan Hageman, private collection
Larry McKee, private collection
Dr. Paul Johnson, private collection
Brian and Terrie Seech, private collection